Money does not have to be the hardest thing you do at church.

There *is* an alternative to nonstop fundraising, convincing people to give more—or simply cutting the budget. This approach lets you discover what you bring to church finances *that you already have,* rather than simply teaching you the latest fundraising technique.

Learn how you can:

- become more thoughtful about the financial challenges you and your church face

- see money—and your own leadership strategies—from a different perspective

- bring more calm and creativity to recurring and unexpected problems in funding ministry

- concentrate on long-term ministry goals and strategic persistence to get financial support for those goals

- focus on yourself and what you can impact directly rather than trying harder to convince others to give more or make different financial decisions

- enjoy the stewardship process rather than dreading it each year

- reduce your overall stress about church finance.

Online Resources

Download these bonus materials to support your reading at
www.margaretmarcuson.com/moneyandyourministry:

- ◆ Money and Your Ministry Journal for chapter questions
- ◆ Additional tips on money and ministry.

For many more free articles on money and on church
leadership, see **www.margaretmarcuson.com/blog**.

E-mail Margaret your feedback and questions
about this book at: **Margaret@margaretmarcuson.com**

Facebook page: **Money and Your Ministry**
Twitter @Marcuson

About the author

The Reverend Margaret Marcuson is a speaker, writer, and
mentor on church leadership, and works across denominations and around North America as consultant and coach on
church leadership and money matters. She served as pastor
of the First Baptist Church of Gardner, Massachusetts for
thirteen years. She now lives in Portland, Oregon.

www.margaretmarcuson.com

For a free conversation about church finance or church
leadership, e-mail her at Margaret@margaretmarcuson.com
or call / text 503-701-7621.

Praise for *Money and Your Ministry:*

In *Money and Your Ministry,* Margaret Marcuson skillfully identifies attitudes and actions that continually thwart church financial flourishing without well-meaning pastors and congregants ever knowing how or why. Marcuson effectively shows us, through case studies and careful observation, how learning more about what we believe and how we behave regarding money is the key to intentionally embracing money as a divine blessing, rather than softly dreading it as a necessary bother—if not evil. I found this to be a faithful, meaningful, and even fun read!

> — KIRK BYRON JONES, author of
> *Fulfilled: Living and Leading with Unusual Wisdom, Peace, and Joy*

Readers who come to *Money and Ministry: Balance the Books While Keeping Your Balance* seeking advice on encouraging greater generosity will find it—and more. Margaret Marcuson challenges leaders to consider first their own hearts before seeking to grow the hearts of others. Her message is clear: as goes the pastor's relationship with money, so goes the congregation's.

> — REBEKAH BURCH BASINGER, co-author of
> *Growing Givers' Hearts: Treating Fundraising as Ministry*

This book on money and ministry will not help leaders learn how to read a spreadsheet, create a budget, or analyze endowment account reports. Those are necessary skills to have, certainly. Marcuson, however, presents us with deeper and less talked-about issues related to churches and money. Oriented from a systems theory perspective, Marcuson addresses the matter of money and ministry rarely touched upon: coming to terms with one's relationship with money and how that impacts ministry leadership for stewardship.

Throughout the book Marcuson raises generative questions that will help the reader clarify how her or his relationship with money influences the capacity to provide pastoral leadership for the congregation. Her premise that until the pastoral leader resolves his or her personal issues about money, no amount of fiduciary expertise will have lasting impact on the church's issues about stewardship is "right on the money."

> — ISRAEL GALINDO, *Associate Dean*
> *for Lifelong Learning, Columbia Theological Seminary*

Praise for *Leaders Who Last:*

Leaders Who Last is a must for church leaders who want their position to be more than short term.

— *Midwest Book Review*

Her solid, hard-won, sometimes playful teaching can refresh a weary pastor just by reading.

— DR. HEATHER ENTREKIN *on Ethicsdaily.com*

Leaders Who Last is a must read for leaders who take themselves too seriously and/or have the knack for making others dependent on them. It is an excellent training tool for young ministers and a good refresher course for experienced—and perhaps frustrated—ministers.

— *Baptists Today*

Money and Your Ministry

MONEY
AND YOUR
MINISTRY

Balance the Books While
Keeping Your Balance

MARGARET J. MARCUSON

Marcuson Leadership Circle
Portland, Oregon

Library of Congress Control Number: 2013917821
ISBN: 978-0-9764366-4-5

Published by Marcuson Leadership Circle
3439 NE Sandy Blvd. #102
Portland, Oregon 97232
www.margaretmarcuson.com

Printed in the United States of America.

This book is for Cindy,
who first invited me to join her in Edwin Friedman's
training program. Thanks for all the talks about money,
ministry, family, and life for the last twenty years and more.

Table of Contents

Foreword

"THE LOVE OF MONEY," we are told, "is the root of all evil." Money is also the source of much anxiety. No doubt, the two have much to do with one another. Margaret Marcuson's ability to handle money issues reflectively and calmly, and to urge readers to do the same, is a mark of this work. In discussing money, she combines a biblical/theological perspective with the lens of Bowen family systems theory, both of which speak of a non-anxious approach to monetary issues. Marcuson breaks the strong taboo to keep talk to a minimum about money in the church. She is not preachy, but gives witness to her beliefs; she is not legalistic, yet takes a position.

What drew my attention immediately was what Marcuson has to say about Bowen theory. I began to think about how my family informed and shaped my view of money. "Don't let it burn a hole in your pocket" was a typical refrain, though I was urged to spend my money carefully and patiently. Stretch your dollars was another instruction: "Money does not grow on trees." Both family axioms contain the message of scarcity. Still, the grand theme rested in the statement "Money cannot buy happiness." Happiness is not a consumer good. Having does not always correlate with being. So I was taught to be frugal and to find contentment beyond material things. A sense of gratitude and an expectation of responsibility were associated with money. None of these came readily, but all were worthy of my attention and action.

Besides helping us to focus on our family system, Marcuson is adept at assisting readers to understand money and personal functioning. She offers case studies to illustrate such things as overfunctioning and triangling with regard to money. Self-regulation is here being given its primary role in our behavioral repertoire. We know from neurological studies that if we do not corral our anxiety, we will be at the mercy of the lower, automatic brain, which is quick to the draw. Then, instead of being thoughtful about money, we let instinct prevail.

Throughout the book, Marcuson takes on the questions often asked about money in the church in a logical and fair manner. Her openness in itself is a model for how we all could deal with money issues in the church and in our families. Silence and secrecy have a lot to do with anxiety. We can all benefit from her urging to look first at our own relationship with money, and from there consider the matter in conversation with others. I am sure those who are interested in exploring stewardship in anxious times will find this volume to be extremely pertinent.

Oh, yes. Marcuson notes that the love of money can be the ground for evil. She knows that money can certainly be an obstacle for ministry and mission in the church. But for the believer, it can also be more. It is a gift; it is a blessing. And who can be anxious about that?

— PETER L. STEINKE

chapter one

Know What You Believe About Money

Money is a gift that passes through us. But the very
first gift that passes through us—through each one of
you and through me—is life itself. Our very existence
is a gift, of which we are temporary keepers.

— Roger Jones, "Money, Anxiety, and Abundance"[1]

IN RECENT YEARS, church leaders' worries about money, as well as real bottom-line financial struggles in congregations, have skyrocketed. Money has always been an anxiety-producing matter in church life and institutional survival has faced challenges before, but it all seems harder now. Churches have laid off staff. Some clergy have seen not merely stagnant salaries but actual pay cuts. Students who entered seminary with a hopeful sense of call have graduated with heavy debt and few job possibilities. Whatever your denomination, and whether your title is pastor, rector, minister, assistant, administrator, or church treasurer, you probably know the familiar realities behind this story, which have led so many of us to increased worry about church finances.

David, a Lutheran pastor, had been at his parish for ten years. He had been preaching about money and cajoling people to support the budget for most of those years. He felt like the grind was endless: council meetings that ended up in a wrangle about the financial reports. The president complaining to him about the treasurer. The increasing budget challenges every year. It was wearing him down. The recession had hit the church budget hard. They had cut back some staff, which meant more work for him. He was tired. Burned out? No, he didn't think so. He noticed, though, he had dreaded coming back from his last vacation and facing the financial reports.

What has been going on in your church lately regarding money and ministry? Like this pastor, you may be worn out by the ongoing worry about whether there will be enough. Or you may be in the middle of a budget crisis that is keeping you awake at night. Or, conversely, you may be facing a windfall that seems like a blessing but also raises questions about how your church makes decisions about money. The question is: *How can church leaders respond to these challenges in ways that give life both to them and to their churches?*

WHAT TO EXPECT

This book is about our relationship with money, and our relationship with other people around money. Here's what you can expect:

♦ You will see ways to become more thoughtful about money in your own life and in the life of your church.

♦ You will learn how to respond to immediate and ongoing financial challenges with greater calm and clarity.

♦ You will find new ways to provide a theological and spiritual foundation for money matters at church.

♦ You will identify ways of relating to others who are anxious about finances and church survival without being thrown off track from your own and the church's vision and purpose.

This approach to financial life is grounded in Bowen family systems theory, especially as expressed by Rabbi Edwin Friedman, who applied Murray Bowen's way of thinking about families to church life. If these ideas are new to you, you can learn some of the basics of family systems thinking and how they apply to church finance. Whether you know a little or a lot about systems theory, you will learn more about how systems thinking can help with a high-anxiety area of ministry and of life: money. We will focus less on the nuts and bolts of church financial life (stewardship techniques, for example) and more on the bigger picture of how you manage yourself in relation to money and other people. When you manage yourself better, you can think and act more effectively around the practicalities of money.

In the pages of this book you will meet some clergy who have struggled with these issues in congregational life and in their own lives, and who have worked hard to lead in this area in recent years. And you will find some practical suggestions and questions to help you in your own life and leadership in church finance. In addition, you will find some specific ways to ground your life with money in your life of faith and prayer.

START WITH THE BIBLE

First, let us begin by considering some biblical and theological bases for our discussion of money. In most of our churches most of the time, we tend to assume that we do not have enough money. Even if we have enough right now, we are not sure we will have enough at the end of the year, or next year. Our vision is short-term. Practically speaking, we typically plan only one year at a time, and sigh with relief if the numbers balance or are close to even. And then we worry that the money pledged won't come in next year. Yet the Bible has a different perspective. Throughout Scripture, from the bounty of Eden and the manna in the wilderness to Revelation's tree of life bearing twelve kinds of fruit, God provides enough and more than enough. The invitation is to trust, with gratitude and celebration—both now and into eternity.

Still, we are inevitably part of institutions that need not just manna but also money to open the doors week by week for worship and for the rest of our ministries. Our church has workers who need to be paid, from the clergy to the custodian. We want to deal with the practicalities of ministry while staying grounded in the scriptural story that has shaped us. Scripture gives us a foundation for examining other ideas that can help us make sense of this thorny topic. To help us think theologically about money, I suggest we begin with a couple of biblical texts, familiar passages that are not often used to consider money matters: Luke 5:1–11 (the miraculous catch of fish) and Philippians 2:5–11 (sometimes called the *kenosis* passage).

◆ Luke 5:1–11

> When [Jesus] had finished speaking, he said to Simon, "Put out into the deep water and let down your nets for a catch." Simon answered, "Master, we have worked all night long but have caught nothing. Yet if you say so, I will let down the nets." When they had done this, they caught so many fish that their nets were beginning to break. (Luke 5:4–6)

In this passage, the call of the disciples in Luke, the disciples felt like they were "fished out." They had been working all night, and they had caught nothing. There were no more resources. But then, when Peter cast the nets out again at Jesus' direction, they are filled to overflowing. It was out of that experience of Jesus' abundance that those first disciples followed him.

Likewise, in our ministries and our churches we can feel like we are fished out—and particularly with money. There isn't enough left, not enough energy, not enough people—and certainly not enough money. We just do not know what to do. We, too, have decided to follow Jesus—and sometimes, after the fact, it seems like we have been working all night and catching nothing. We simply don't have enough money to carry on the ministry we have been called to do.

Or maybe we do have enough: we have an overabundance, a surplus, and we do not quite know what to do with it. It's threatening to sink our boat as we wrangle about decisions. We may say, like Peter, "Go away from me, Lord, for I am a sinful man" (Luke 5:8). We do not feel up to the task at hand, to fulfilling the call we have been given, especially when it comes to dealing with the worldly, risky business of money at church. But, as with Peter, the calling persists even when we feel inadequate.

The promise of this gospel passage is that God will provide what we need—although not always in the way we expect. Peter expected neither the catch of fish nor the call. Like him, we can expect to be surprised along the way. One Baptist pastor of a small congregation has found himself surprised over and over again through twenty years of ministry in that place—particularly by the way God has provided when he has let go. Just when it seems like the church can no longer support its ministry, something new happens: a surprise gift, new members who turn out to be generous givers, and most recently a very large unexpected legacy (which offers its own challenges).

◆ *Philippians 2:5–11*

> Let the same mind be in you that was in Christ Jesus,
>> who, though he was in the form of God,
>> did not regard equality with God
>> as something to be exploited,
>> but emptied himself,
>> taking the form of a slave, being born in human likeness.
>
> And being found in human form,
>> he humbled himself
>> and became obedient to the point of death—
>> even death on a cross. (Philippians 2:6–8)

The second passage is from one of the most ancient Christian hymns, found in Paul's letter to the Philippians. It describes Christ letting go of everything, taking the form of a slave and humbling himself to the point of death. "Therefore," the hymn continues, "God also highly exalted him and gave him the name that is above every name" (2:9). Reflection on Jesus' ultimate letting go can help us as we deal with our anxieties about money; spiritual freedom is the ability to have everything or to have nothing. We can do more than we thought with what we have, and we have more than we thought. We so often think our resources are not adequate to the task. Yet according to this earliest Christian hymn, Jesus divested in a radical way. He gave up his divine form. He gave up his heavenly security. Having embraced human life, he even gave that up, on the cross. There was a price to be paid, and he was willing to pay it. And against all odds and all hope, he received his life back. Jesus' story can encourage us to live out of hope, not out of fear. Fear is not what God wants for us. We need to be smart and careful and use the skills that the world has to offer, but if we live out of fear, we will not be living out of God's will for us and for our churches.

Paul introduces this ancient hymn by talking about humility: "Let the same mind be in you that was in Christ Jesus" (2:5). If we are humble in our dealings with each other around money we will all be better off—mainly by recognizing that it is not "our" money. We do not gain our identity from how much we have. The money that we have, give, or manage for the church is not ours at all. When we are too closely identified with the money, we are in trouble. We cannot be spiritually and emotionally free, we cannot let go of fear, if we are too attached to our money, if we think that who we are is dependent on the money. Rather, the Scripture tells us that God, not our resources, gives us our identity.

We must also acknowledge that in other parts of the Bible, we do find mixed messages about money. David Miller points out the tensions in both the Hebrew and Christian Scriptures. There is one strand that "describes wealth as a blessing, a blessing that God wants to shower upon us with abundance. There is another voice that describes wealth as an obstacle to faith, and a danger."[2] Abraham the patriarch and David the king both have untold wealth, a sign of God's favor, yet the prophets denounce the abuses of the rich. Jesus suggests that it is easier for someone rich to go through the eye of the needle than to get into heaven, yet women of means supported his ministry and Joseph of Arimathea, a rich man, provided Jesus' own tomb. The early Christians were largely drawn from the lower levels of society, yet there were also key patrons such as Lydia, a successful businesswoman. As Miller points out, even the gospels show a varied perspective on the views of Jesus himself: Is it "Blessed are the poor in spirit" (Matthew 5:3) or "Blessed are you who are poor" (Luke 6:20)?[3] These texts mirror our own experience of money as gift and difficulty, blessing and evil.

These various threads in Scripture have been teased out and used by people to support their own theological, political, and practical ends. Strands within the church have viewed money both as dangerous, even evil, and as a sign of God's blessing. From St. Peter's Basilica to St. Francis of Assisi, the Christian church has run the gamut from luxurious indulgence to outright rejection of riches. In our day, prosperity preachers call the faithful to claim their "due" and urban intentional communities embrace simplicity. Faithful Christians still struggle with the question, how do we best relate to money? Through the church's history there have always been people who understood God's generosity. There have also been those who lived out of fear of scarcity or grasped for all they could get. The theological foundation I want to lay for this book is that of God's love and provision for all our needs, so that you can be free (or freer) from anxiety about money. You can navigate better the inevitable tension if you are freer and less fearful. You can recognize that it does not all depend on you. The theme of divine generosity runs through Scripture from beginning to end.

LEARNING FROM THE CHURCH'S STORY

In addition to using Scripture as a resource, we can look through the centuries of the church's history to find strength as we face the challenge of dealing with money. Far from being a dead past, this history offers still relevant commentary on the thorny matter of money and possessions. The struggle of putting money into perspective is nothing new for Christians. Here are three ways the church has related to money through the centuries that can be helpful to us today.

◆ Total trust in God

The first way is to have total trust in God. From those who took a vow of poverty to those who have given 10 percent and more of their income to those who have devoted their lives to the church, there have always been Christians who understood that God is the source of all that is and were able to live that way, both institutionally and personally. This was and continues to be the great strength for the church. Leaders and members who are freely devoted make the church more resilient and resourceful.

Christian leaders and teachers have recognized how important it is to keep our hearts open to know and receive God's provision. The monastic movement from the fourth century on called those who joined to take a vow of poverty as a way of living out this trust. Much later, Martin Luther famously spoke of the conversion of the heart, the conversion of the mind, and the conversion of the pocketbook. He understood that coming to this point can be a real challenge, saying that the third conversion was the most difficult. We must remember that the conversion of the pocketbook, like the other conversions, is not once-and-for-all, but an ongoing spiritual practice.

What does this mean for us in our ministry and in our relationship with our church resources? We may choose to be proactive in asking more of our congregations, but we can still live out of trust. We can trust that God will care for us and for our churches. Does this mean we will automatically meet this budget or build that building? No, of course not. But it means we do not need to walk through our ministries in fear or anxiety. We can make all of our decisions in total trust in God's love and provision. We will make different decisions if we do so.

◆ Put money in its place
The second way is keeping money in its appropriate place. Those who have viewed money as a tool, not a value in itself, have always done better in life and in ministry. Those who make it the ultimate value (whether accumulating it or rejecting it) can get into trouble spiritually, and often institutionally. Many of the worst abuses in Christian history come from an up-ending of values, with money and its attendant power becoming more important than they should be.

Trusting in money rather than in God has been viewed as idolatry from the earliest days of the church. The earliest Christian writers had plenty to say about the spiritual dangers of wealth. Clement of Alexandria, for example, suggested that believers should be willing to give up their possessions if they get in the way of their Christian life.[4] Another early church leader, Augustine of Hippo, suggested that when we make money an intrinsic value, "it becomes an idol in place of God. When we treat it instrumentally, it can be a facility for a life centered on God."[5] When we keep money in its appropriate place, viewing it as a tool rather than the source of our security, we have more freedom.

We can be overly attached to our money (or to not having money, for that matter). John Calvin called for a balanced approach to "mistaken strictness and mistaken laxity," adding, "If we must simply pass through this world, there is no doubt we ought to use its good things in so far as they help rather than hinder our course. Thus Paul rightly persuades us to use this world as if not using it; and to buy goods with the same attitude as one sells them."[6] As Christians and church leaders living in today's society, we use money and the things it buys every day. The more freedom and flexibility we have as money comes and goes, the better we will be able to serve God and the church.

It is not just about the money, of course, but about the larger purpose of God's work in the world and in us. When we remember this, we do not get so focused on the money and our fear that there won't be enough. Money is a resource and it is risky. The church has always known this, and consequently we can see there have been trends toward both asceticism and greed throughout its history. What does it mean for the church, local and universal, to have enough? I think the two strands, of extreme greed and extreme asceticism, are both signs of anxiety. Money itself is neither devilish nor heavenly; it can be used as a tool for evil and for good. At its worst it has been a tool of overwhelming ambition, greed, and exploitation, even in the church. At its best it has been used in the life of the church to accomplish God's work in the world. Keeping perspective on money means we can allow it to flow into and out of our lives as grace.

One method of keeping money in perspective has to do with the fundamentals of good management. According to the gospels, even the twelve disciples had a treasurer, so we can assume that the practicalities of dealing with money in ministry do matter. Joan Chittister notes in her book *The Rule of Benedict* that the spiritual life is not "an excuse to ignore the things of the world, to go through time suspended above the mundane, to lurch from place to place with a balmy head and a saccharine smile on the face." Avoiding idolatry does not mean we avoid the necessary tasks related to money and ministry. Chittister suggests that Benedictine spirituality is as much about "good order, wise management, and housecleaning" as it is about contemplation.[7] Even those who take a vow of poverty understand this. Likewise, in the local church it is vitally important to do the work of raising adequate funds and managing them well. It does take money to do ministry, and that money needs to be administered well. Giving money *enough* attention is just as important as not giving it too much.

◆ *Sacrificial giving*
The third way that the church has related to money over the centuries is, of course, its focus on the importance of sacrificial giving. This belief has consistently formed part of the church's teaching about money. Giving has been as an essential element in the task of keeping money in perspective. In his second letter to the church in Corinth, Paul writes with admiration about the generosity of the churches of Macedonia: "During a severe ordeal of affliction, their abundant joy and their extreme poverty have overflowed in a wealth of generosity on their part. For, as I can testify, they voluntarily gave according to their means, and even beyond their means" (2 Cor. 8:2–3). He challenges the church in Corinth likewise to share generously in an offering for the Jerusalem church, which was perennially in need.

Following Paul's example, Christians through the centuries have given their money to the church and to those in need as part of their faith and practice. Luther suggested that those who have received God's grace can "most freely and most willingly" spend themselves and all their money in the service of others.[8] Barbara Owen notes, "Money and love are connected, Luther thought. When we realize how much God loves us, we will want to give as God gives. 'If I have won someone's heart, I will soon have his purse too,' he said."[9] Elsewhere, Luther picturesquely said, "When he sees a man who has no coat, he says to his money: 'Come out, young Mr. Gulden! There is a poor naked man who has no coat; you must serve him. Over there lies a sick man who has no refreshment. Come forth, Sir Dollars! You must be on your way; go and help.'"[10] Giving to the church and to those in need are values that run through the centuries. Every Christian generation has to reaffirm these values for itself. John Wesley, the founder of Methodism, famously preached in a sermon on "The Use of Money" that "we ought to gain all we can gain but this it is certain we ought not to do; we ought not to gain money at the expense of life, nor at the expense of our health," and that "having, first, gained all you can, and, secondly, saved all you can, then 'give all you can.'"[11]

KEEPING OUR PERSPECTIVE ABOUT MONEY

As we try to manage both the flow of money into and out of our churches and our lives, and also our own relationship with that flow, there is a way forward. It isn't always an easy way. It requires prayer and self-reflection and hard conversations, as well as time on the clock and on the calendar. But I am convinced that it is possible to have greater freedom in regard to money and in our relationships with each other about money, to have fewer sleepless nights and wrangling meetings. Put simply, our goal is to have more money to do the work of God in the world and more vision to draw that money into our ministries. This goal is possible because the Holy Spirit is at work in all of our churches, in all the varied stages of the life journey of congregations, from church plants to those deciding it is time to close their doors. And the Spirit is at work in us, workaday church leaders who are trying our best to make decisions that are in the best interest of the church. We are part of ordinary local churches that are attempting to figure out ministry in the twenty-first century and how to continue to support it financially. We are Christians who are trying to make a connection between our faith and our resources. And we are all trying to keep perspective on our resources in an age when we may seem to have less than we used to, but still have far more than almost everyone on the planet. Stepping back to maintain a global perspective can help us lighten up about our own fears about our lack of resources.

We can begin the process by holding all that we have lightly, accepting the flow. We don't clasp our hands tightly—whether around our "own" possessions and money, or the building and resources of the congregation or the wider church of which we are a part. This open-handed stance enables us to receive as a gift the resources we have and to give beyond our own needs, as individuals and as a community; it allows us to give and to receive freely. Most of us need a lifetime to work on moving toward greater freedom in relation to money and things and the choices we make about them, but we can start simply where we are, with what we have been given.

Finally, viewing money not only from the perspective of the Bible and theology but also with the lens of family systems thinking can give us some tools for walking through the thorny lanes of the endless conversations about money at church. What does family systems thinking have to do with theology? Or with the Bible? Beginning with Adam and Eve in the garden, the Bible is about relationships. So a way of thinking about life that addresses relationships, as family systems theory does, is right on target for us in the church. All of creation is about relationship, as scientists seem to be discovering more and more each day. God created the universe—and us—for relationship. In fact, money itself is about relationships. If we didn't need to relate to each other, we wouldn't have money. Money was invented by human beings, and we use it with each other. One of the things money symbolizes, for better and for worse, is human connection.

Using this perspective, we can understand why those money conversations so often go wrong, and how to do better with them. We can see why and how money becomes an automatic focus for our anxiety and that of others. Those fights about money are not "about" money at all, but about position and power and history and relationships. How do we do better with it? By taking the time to think through our own fundamental faith principles about ministry and about money, what we want for ourselves and for our congregations, and how we need to be present with others in these difficult conversations. And by learning how to be less caught up with our own anxiety and the anxiety of others. There are not only theological but systemic reasons for the historical views of money in the church through the ages, and our struggles in the present. Because money is an automatic focus for anxiety, and because of its connection with survival, families and institutions pay a lot of attention to money. When we can pay more *thoughtful* attention to money matters, we will both have better relationships with others and make better choices for the present and for the future.

The theological and the theoretical dimensions to money issues are important, but not enough. Practically speaking, churches face a variety of specific challenges related to money. Here are some examples of the dilemmas that can arise, which we will look at in greater detail in the next chapter.

◆ In one suburban Baptist church, overall giving has gone down due to the deaths of several generous givers, and a budget gap means staff must be reduced. Leaders are struggling with balancing the needs of staff and the realities of the budget, while keeping in mind the relationships the staff members have developed within the congregation. Should they eliminate a single position or reduce all the salaries equally? Should they listen to the supporters of certain staff members who are advocating to retain them? Or is there some way to avoid decreasing staff by increasing giving, and thus maintain the paid ministry at its current level?

◆ A member of a small Lutheran church has left the congregation a large legacy, and leaders disagree about how to use it. Family members of the deceased also have opinions. The gift is unrestricted, and some members think it should be used for necessary repairs. Others want the church to set aside a larger portion for mission and outreach.

◆ The pastor of an urban Presbyterian church does not want to talk about money, and the lay leadership is frustrated. He agrees he should do more, but can never seem to force himself to step up when it's time. He reluctantly gives a stewardship sermon every fall, and he feels the pressure to do more, but money matters just make him anxious.

◆ The treasurer of a growing Methodist church, a long-time member, is suspected of embezzling funds, after the new minister with a financial background noticed some discrepancies and began asking questions. Leaders do not want to offend the treasurer by looking into it, and his family gives substantially to the church.

◆ An Episcopal church with a declining membership has an old building, which takes up a significant portion of the budget, leaving little for program or outreach. The rector would like to take the opportunity to buy a nearby building which would serve their needs better, but long-time members are strongly committed to maintaining the old building.

Any one of these cases might arise in your church. What would you do? There are no quick fixes or easy answers, but leaders can thoughtfully walk through these challenges and the many others that arise in relation to money. We will discuss possible responses in chapter two, and examine some of the basics of systems thinking that can help us deal with a variety of dilemmas we face in our financial lives at church and at home.

People approach books differently, but here are a few suggestions for how to use this book:

◆ Read the book straight through.

◆ Read chapter two next, and then whatever chapter interests you the most.

◆ Jot down a few notes in answer to the questions in each chapter, or two or three of the questions.

◆ Read a chapter a day, and then think about it until the next day.

◆ Talk with someone about what you are reading.

◆ Most importantly, *focus on yourself* and how you can shift your own relationship with money, rather than thinking about how other people (spouse, staff, church leaders, the congregation as a whole) might change.

To sum up, this book addresses your most important resource in leading around money: yourself. When church leaders can stay clear-headed about themselves and their own goals, even in a financial crunch or crisis, churches will do better, and the ministry is much more likely to continue on an even keel. We do not know what the economic future will hold, yet the church will continue, God's work will continue, our calling will remain.

IDEAS TO PONDER

What do you want for your church? Think for a moment. What do you want for your church, for its finances, for the people within as they relate to their resources? Take a moment right now and write down your thoughts. Save these notes, and take a look at them again after you have read this book. What if God wants you to want more than you've dared to imagine for yourself or for your church? Greater freedom, less attachment to the money you have. Maybe more giving of yourself—or maybe less. God wants you, and me, and all of us together to be free. Stop now, and write down what you want.

◆ *Questions*

Here are seven more questions to begin to consider yourself as you relate to money:

1. How would you describe your relationship with money?

2. What is your current biggest challenge in regard to money?

3. What do you want for yourself in this relationship with money?

4. What is enough for you? For your church?

5. What are some ways money might be a blessing?

6. Is there something in regard to money you would like to let go of?

7. How does your faith affect your money choices?

chapter two

Understand the Meaning of Money

I think of money as if it were a lightning rod.
Wherever our anxiety is, it's bound to be somewhere
near the money. And those who are near the money tend
to take on a significant amount of this anxiety, whether
that is pastor or treasurer or endowment committee.

— Bob Hunter, former Director of Stewardship,
Second Presbyterian Church, Indianapolis[1]

IN THIS CHAPTER, we will consider how a family systems perspective on congregational life can help leaders better
understand the challenges and find their way through the thorny
paths of church finance. We will examine in more detail several
cases of specific churches facing money challenges, looking at
systemic issues as well as questions of authority and governance.
Church leaders can find immediate help in financial issues by
finding a way to step back and approach their challenges
thoughtfully.

THE MEANING OF MONEY

It is not enough simply to pay attention to the nuts and bolts of
church financial life. Of course, bills must be paid. Staff must
receive their salaries. The endowment must be managed. Budgeting must be done. The funds must be raised somehow. How-

ever, it is easy to spend a lot of time on crucial matters of church finance and still be blindsided because we do not pay enough attention to the emotional side of money. When we look only at the numbers and disregard the system of relationships in the congregation, in the present and over time, we will never have a real handle on what is at work in our church.

Remember, money is never simply about money. It goes much deeper: it's also about relationships, about the give and take between people. These connections involve what systems theory calls *emotional process*: not the surface feelings, but the instinctive side of human life, the way we react rather than respond to one another. It's easy to have a mindless reaction when money is involved. You bypass the reflective part of your brain, and find yourself in survival mode. The fight-or-flight response has kicked in. Suddenly, in the middle of the council meeting, you can't think clearly about the budget conversation. You go home kicking yourself because you didn't speak up to defend the outreach budget, but simply let them slash it to the bone.

SYSTEMS BASICS ABOUT MONEY

How do we get more reflective about our experiences with money? Let us begin by looking at some of the basics of systems thinking and how they work in relation to finances. Next, we will apply them to specific congregations and their financial situations.

◆ *Anxiety*

As one pastor said, "It always seems to have an exclamation point when money is involved." Money easily becomes a focus for people's anxiety. Edwin Friedman used to say that the issue is never the issue. In other words, we think the argument is about money. But instead, people simply focus their anxiety on the issue at hand, and money is often that issue. Money has to do with survival—personal and institutional—so it easily draws our anxious attention. This ongoing chronic anxiety around survival shows up in a variety of forms in congregational life. Here are some of the ways:

◆ Secrecy around money.

◆ Denial around financial realities—thinking there isn't enough when there is, or thinking there is enough when there isn't.

◆ Overestimating or underestimating giving capacity.

◆ Regular "crises" around finances, real or imagined.

◆ Embezzlement or mismanagement.

◆ Resisting necessary expenses like deferred maintenance.

◆ High reactivity around the way church leadership raises funds.

◆ Never talking about money or, conversely, always talking about money.

◆ Blind trust in the leadership around money matters, or, conversely, extreme suspicion of leadership.

◆ *Overfunctioning and underfunctioning*

There's a reciprocal relationship between those who take too much responsibility and those who do not take enough responsibility. In congregational life, there are always those who give more / worry more / spend more time on the money than others. In systems theory this is called *overfunctioning*. Members who are overfunctioning with financial aspects of the church always think if others gave more or were more responsible, the church wouldn't have this problem. Yet there's a balance between those who overfunction and those who underfunction in terms of financial responsibility. It takes both to keep this overresponsible / underresponsible dynamic going.

Often key church leaders carry the anxiety for church finances. Who is staying awake at night? Typically, it's the pastor, although sometimes lay leaders are more worried than the clergy. I talked recently with a church treasurer who was losing sleep night after night over whether there would be enough money in the account to pay the bills. In this situation, the potential shortfall did not belong to the treasurer but to the church. It wasn't his responsibility—or not his alone. Yet he was the one who was holding all the anxiety for it.

Overfunctioning is driven by anxiety. We feel anxious as to whether others are going to step forward and be responsible, and so we step in, either to help them or to do it ourselves. The basic rule of the overfunctioning–underfunctioning reciprocity, as it's called, is that underfunctioners do not step up to take responsibility until overfunctioners step down. For most of us who were born to be too responsible, this is not easy. And when it's in a high-anxiety area like money, this is even more difficult. It can seem like it's our job (paid or unpaid) to worry, and to do everything we can to make sure the budget balances.

Clergy can also *underfunction* in the area of money. Some ministers do not like to deal with finances or feel inadequate when they see a report. So they leave money matters to the laity. If this is you, recognize your own strengths and weaknesses, but also remember that attention to the financial side of church life is an important basic for pastoral leaders. Underfunctioning, like overfunctioning, is anxiety-driven. If you want to step up your functioning in this area, one way to start is to notice your responses when money is the topic at hand. Awareness is the first step toward making different choices.

◆ Triangles

A triangle occurs when the relationship between two people becomes troubled, and a third person (or group) is pulled in to manage the anxiety between the two. Given the high-octane nature of money in church life, we can expect triangles to show up frequently in this area—and they do, as we will soon see. If you hear comments like, "Don't you agree with me that the pastor is completely wrong about his approach to stewardship?" someone is pulling you into a triangle about money.

Clergy cannot opt out of these triangles; they go with the job. In addition, triangles are not bad in and of themselves: they are part of human experience. However, the way you choose to relate to the other people who are part of the triangles you are in regarding money can contribute to a different outcome. It's easy to get caught up in the anxiety of others around money, yet a thoughtful response will lead to better results than a reactive response. Let us review some of the basics of functioning within the inevitable triangles and see how this can work in practice.

Remember: *you cannot change the "other side" of a triangle.* In other words, you cannot change a relationship you do not belong to. For example, as pastor, you may agree that the board could do more for staff compensation, or you may want to defend the board's decisions to your staff. Yet getting caught up in bemoaning or defending will not help anyone make progress. You can advocate with the board, but you cannot force them to make the budget decisions you want.

In addition, *if you try to change the other side of a triangle, the situation often gets worse.* People resist, consciously or unconsciously, our attempts to change them. In the case just mentioned, you cannot manage the dissatisfaction of your colleagues with the board regarding salaries. At least, you can't do it without adding significantly to your own stress.

Finally, *when you try to change someone else's relationship, you carry the stress that belongs to the other two.* Trying to do the impossible always creates stress. And you relieve them of the necessary responsibility for their own relationship. The only choice we have is how we function within triangles: relating directly to each party, in as clear, open, and consistent a manner as possible. What can you do? You can stay positively connected with staff, communicate neutrally about the work of the board, and provide appropriate support and encouragement in their work. Ultimately, each staff person has to decide whether he or she can live with the compensation being offered, or not.

Secrets about money always involve triangles. Two parties are on the inside and a third is left out. In family life, this might be seen in estate planning. One child knows how the parents are disposing of their assets, and the others do not. At church, the secret might be between the priest and the vestry as to how dire the financial situation is. The congregation doesn't know. They are on the outside of the triangle. This may be all right on a temporary basis, yet if it becomes chronic, it will create problems.

Triangles inevitably emerge when churches have to make hard decisions. People try to recruit others for their side of the issue: "Don't you agree that the board/pastor are right/wrong about these budget changes?" There may be a triangle between the pastor and two factions. Or between the pastor, board, and congregation. Sarah, an Episcopal rector, found that at a vestry meeting one member said, "All we have to do to solve this budget deficit is for Sarah to double the membership." He was intensifying a triangle between the vestry, the rector, and the membership. You need to make your case—define yourself—without frantically lobbying people to agree with you. Anxious recruitment does not lead to thoughtful decision-making. And people resist being coerced even if they like the idea on the table.

In addition, church leaders need to resist the temptation to avoid people who disagree with them on the matter under discussion. Now, more than ever, maintaining relationships is critical. Don't triangle people out by excluding them from key conversations. Don't complain about people who disagree, even if they are behaving badly. If there is a lot of reactivity around the decision, you may need to strategize with key leaders on how to respond, but that is not the same as whining about people's behavior: "I can't believe they...." Do your best to remain calm and clear, defining yourself rather than talking about others.

◆ *Balance*
A church system develops over time a certain balance in its relationships in regard to money. Finances are handled in a particular way, year after year. Perhaps someone always rescues the budget at the end of the year, or, in a financial crisis, everyone pitches in to handle the problem. The church may call pastor after pastor, and none is comfortable talking about money. Or a church may always respond creatively to fund the budget, so they don't see money as a really big issue, even through the Great Depression and many recessions. When leaders seek to change the balance, congregations respond with some kind of "change back" message. It's not personal: it's an automatic systemic response, although it can be framed personally: "Pastor, we've never had a stewardship campaign around here, and we don't need one now."

◆ *Differentiated leadership*

Differentiated leadership has to do with personal maturity: our ability to be clear within ourselves *and* to relate to others (including those who disagree with us) out of that clarity. Those leaders who make a lasting contribution in church finances show up and take responsibility for themselves and their own leadership role in relation to money. Leaders who function this way will be able to say, "Here's what I think about how we should handle this budget situation," without trying to convince or cajole others—and without cutting off or avoiding those who take a different view. They can manage their own emotional reactivity even in the face of the reactivity of others. They care about results, and they don't get their entire identity caught up in their role. They can manage themselves in money matters, and relate to others who are anxious about money, in a culture which also has high anxiety in this area. This is not an easy task. Yet even a small increase in your ability to do this will make a big difference in your experience of ministry, and even in the church's financial life.

The top leader holds a key position in the church system. When that leader functions maturely, money matters are likely to go better overall: giving will be stronger and financial challenges will be solved more easily. The leader needs to be present, especially at times of uncertainty, crisis, and transition. Pastors, rectors, and senior ministers ideally seek to stay calm no matter what is going on in the congregation's finances. And they work to stay in touch with other key leaders and with the congregation, in as many ways as possible.

Nevertheless, even the best, most mature leadership is not magic. Functioning in this way does not necessarily guarantee the financial results you want. Parish money life includes many variables: the congregation's history, the emotional maturity and financial well-being of the current membership, the wider economy. My grandmother used to say, "Do your best: angels can't do better." I suggest the same approach to leading your congregation in this area of church finance: Do your best, and let go of the rest.

FIVE CASES ABOUT MONEY

Now we will examine five churches from different denominations that are facing several different financial challenges, to see how the above ideas apply, given various structures. These principles operate in different church contexts, no matter how the authority structure is established. Still, it is important to pay attention to governance matters as you think through ways of responding to the inevitable challenges that emerge over time.

◆ *Case 1. Reduced giving*

First, let's look at a suburban Baptist church facing reduced giving, which will likely lead to staff reductions. Several significant givers have died, and the newer, younger members are not giving at the same level. The pastor and the board of deacons will have to make a recommendation to the congregation for a vote. (Note: Baptist churches vary in the nature of the governing board. For some the board is comprised of deacons, for others the trustees, and for still others it is a council made up of the chairpersons of all standing committees.) There are significant differences in standing among the staff: the associate pastor was called by the congregation, and can only be dismissed by a congregational vote, while the remaining staff was hired by the board. A charismatic and popular youth director is one staff member. A music director who has had ongoing conflicts with the pastor is another. The other staff, with secretarial and custodial duties, are already part-time. Parents and choir members have gotten wind of possible reductions and are lobbying the pastor and moderator for their favorites.

In congregational polity, the church as a whole has the final authority to approve the budget. In this church the pastor has key positional authority, but she cannot make the decision. The finance committee develops a budget which the deacons approve and send to the congregation for final approval. It's always important to think through clearly how the decision will be made. Who has the authority to make it, and what is the process by which it will be made? Here, the congregation makes the final decision. Yet leadership can and should be exercised by the pastor, the finance chair, and the chair of the deacons and/or the moderator (some Baptist churches have both; some have a moderator who takes both roles). They each need to do some clear thinking separately and together about what is in the best interests of the church's ministry. They will make some decisions about what to recommend to the next body which will discuss the matter. And they need to strategically present their recommendations at each step along the way. For example, the finance committee can have a thoughtful discussion about the challenge, under the leadership of the chair, and say to the deacons, "Here's what we'd like to see happen."

In addition to these questions about structure and authority, it is important for this pastor and other key leaders to recognize the emotional process at work. As noted earlier, even the best procedures can be undercut if these elements are not taken into account. Leaders can recognize that this is a time of high anxiety for the congregation as a whole. This anxiety naturally focuses on the money itself, as well as on youth and music ministry (both typical places where anxiety gets directed in congregations). At times such as this, leaders have a particular responsibility to stay calm themselves.

Leaders can notice there are a number of triangles at play right off the bat: the supporters of various staff members are beginning to triangle in the finance committee. The finance chair received numerous conflicting voicemails and e-mails the day of the committee meeting to discuss possible staff reductions. If the chair or important members of the committee begin to get anxious about this, it will be harder for them to think clearly. When someone triangles in another person, they are typically trying to manage their own anxiety by dumping it on someone else. The committee members risk finding themselves overly caught up in what other people are thinking. They need to take the time to discern what their own best thinking is, individually and collectively.

What might leaders do about these triangles? First of all, the pastor might simply recognize the triangles for what they are. When someone approaches her with an opinion, she can listen, without feeling like she must relieve all their anxieties. She might neutrally comment, "It's a difficult process for everyone." The finance chair in turn might respond to calls and e-mails, thanking these individuals for their input without getting too involved in a back-and-forth discussion of what the committee should or shouldn't do.

The pastor may have an opinion about what decisions should be made, and she can clearly state them in the appropriate settings. She might say to the finance committee or the board of deacons, "I'd like to see us make a big push to increase giving rather than starting out by cutting the budget." Or, "I think we're going to have to cut the budget, and I think this will be a good time to make some staff changes we've needed to make for some time." It's important for her to ask herself, "What do I want?" and get as clear as she can at the time. Then she can say, "Here's what I think," or, "Here's what I would like to see happen." The pastor needs to recognize that this is the church's decision, and she cannot control the outcome. This is one kind of triangle: the pastor, the church, and its future. Letting go of the "other side" of the triangle means being free of too much attachment to a particular outcome. It is their decision, not hers.

The same is true for key lay leaders; they also need to be clear about the extent of their authority. It is overfunctioning to carry more responsibility than they actually have. If you are a lay leader, don't overstep the bounds of authority of what your committee or board can do. Once you have made an appropriate decision, don't lie awake worrying about matters you cannot control, such as what other people choose to pledge or give, or whether people get upset about your board's decision.

Here's one possible step-by-step scenario. First, the pastor meets with the finance committee chair. She coaches him not to panic, but to keep his wits about him and his sense of humor intact. Then, at the finance committee meeting, the pastor and the chair work together to maintain a sense of positive solution-gathering, not gloom and doom, while acknowledging the challenge at hand. They develop a first draft of a possible budget, focusing on ministry priorities rather than simply going through line items. The pastor and the finance chair then meet with the moderator, explaining where the finance committee is coming from. The moderator may be skeptical at first, but after a conversation she understands each of their positions. The pastor stays in frequent touch with both before the deacons' meeting. The budget recommends reducing rather than eliminating the positions of both the choir director and the youth director, to honor the congregation's expressed ministry priorities of a focus on dynamic worship and vital youth ministry. It also includes a recommendation for a year-round stewardship program rather than a once-a-year appeal, at the pastor's suggestion.

The pastor also decides to start working with the personnel committee to clarify a better review process for all staff, and to pay more attention to her relationship with both the youth and music staff members. She recognizes that her relationship problems with the music minister have colored the budget conversations more than they should have. Churches often use budget challenges as an excuse to get rid of someone when they haven't had the courage to address performance matters along the way.

At the deacons' meeting, deacons who are choir members and those who are youth parents begin to argue with each other, but the moderator stays calm, and focuses their attention on the wider ministry of the church rather than specific programs. They review the budget at a first reading, and as usual decide to bring it up at the next meeting for final approval. By the time the budget is presented to the congregation, the leadership is all in agreement. Questions are raised, especially by vocal choir members, but they are answered calmly and thoroughly. The budget is passed with only a few dissenting votes.

◆ *Case 2. A large legacy*
A small Lutheran congregation has received a legacy of half a million dollars. The church has a modest endowment. There are significant deferred maintenance issues on the building, and members of the property committee want to spend a good part of the money to take care of these. The congregation has also developed a plan for connecting more effectively with their neighborhood, and the outreach team would like some of the legacy to be set aside for a pilot project.

The donor was a member of one of the founding families, which still has a significant presence in the congregation, including an influential past president, the donor's son. He wants to see the money preserved, with any income being designated for the building. Although the gift is unrestricted, he says his mother was very concerned about how run-down the building has become. He and a former pastor had some conflict when he was the president.

The current pastor is well-positioned to influence the decision. He is well-liked, and has been able to help the church move toward a stronger emphasis on mission during his tenure of ten years. Additionally, this church has a history of strong pastors.

In this congregation, the congregation council can make the decision what to do. But they are reluctant to do so without the congregation's support (and, preferably, that of the former president). The current president is anxious, and tells the pastor he is worried that this key family might leave. He wants to go along with the idea to use a chunk of the money for the building, with the remainder invested for future building needs. The pastor had a strong relationship with the deceased, even though he has struggled somewhat in his connection with the son.

The pastor is part of several key triangles in this situation—especially with the current and past presidents. He needs to pay close attention to his pastoral care with the past president, and in his own mind separate this out from the tension over the money. He knows that he needs to always cover the bases of pastoral care, and if he does so, money issues will likely be less intense. The worst thing he can do is avoid this parishioner, both pastorally and strategically. It is always important to remember the link between pastoral care and leadership goals.

Because of the pastor's strong connection with the deceased and with the congregation as a whole, he can influence the decision, but he cannot control it. The council must decide. Since the current president is anxious, the pastor might experiment with coaching him to lead in a calmer way. Or he might simply work to keep himself calm, and lighten up along the way. He might tell himself, "If they decide to go with the building, at least we'll get that roof leak fixed." But he shouldn't hesitate to say what he thinks: "I'd like to see us devote a significant part of this legacy to funding our new outreach program."

In this case, the council decided to use the income from the money for the building but not any of the principal. They did affirm verbally the commitment to outreach, though they were not willing to commit additional funds. The pastor decided not to view it as a giant setback (even though that was his emotional response). He was able to let go of it, and instead chose to focus a portion of his time on the neighborhood outreach and to advocate for the funding in next year's budget process. He was disappointed but didn't take it personally.

◆ *Case 3. A pastor who avoids money talk*
In an urban Presbyterian church, the pastor is reluctant to talk about money. The board, or session, has pressed him to preach about it more, but he doesn't want to. Lay leaders, all sophisticated in financial matters, are anxious about the church's finances. They are starting to talk to each other about their concern about what they perceive as a lack of leadership. The pastor feels like he ought to make himself do more, but he cannot seem to do it.

In almost any system, if the pastor or minister is not interested, it is challenging for lay leaders to make headway. It may be particularly difficult in this church because in Presbyterian polity, the pastor holds the ability to set the agenda and moderates the session meetings. Yet according to the Presbyterian *Book of Order,* the session is responsible for "encouraging the graces of generosity and faithful stewardship" (G-3.0201a), so theoretically at least they do have financial authority.

A key question for volunteer leaders around finance can sometimes be, "How do we get our pastor to address money more openly?" There's a triangle here between the pastor, the leadership, and the congregation about money. Frustrated leaders might continue to work hard on their relationship with the pastor, without trying to get overly willful toward him in this area. They could say more about what they want: "I'd like to see us talk more openly about money." This is leading from below.

The pastor, in turn, might do some reflection on the sources of his discomfort about money matters, particularly his family of origin. He can be clear with key leaders about what he is willing to do, and what he is not willing to do: "I'm willing to try this stewardship program which suggests a three-sermon series on stewardship." "I'd rather not give another stewardship sermon during the year." He can acknowledge his own challenges and their frustration: "I know this isn't my strongest area of ministry, and I'd like to get better at it," without getting anxious or defensive. Over time, he may find himself more comfortable with this part of his ministry.

◆ *Case 4. A matter of embezzlement*
In another case, a growing Methodist church suspects that the treasurer is embezzling funds. The new minister has a financial background, and he has noticed the record-keeping seems sloppy. The end-of-year reports raise even more red flags. He is reluctant to bring this issue to other church leaders, let alone the wider conference, but recognizes he will have to do both soon. He feels his heart in his throat, but he takes a deep breath and begins with a conversation with the council president: "I think there may be some problems with what Bud has done with the money."

In the Methodist structure, the minister is more in the middle than in some other polities. The pastor is accountable to the conference through the district superintendent. So he needs to go to the wider denomination sooner rather than later. The blessing, as the pastor realized, was that he did not have to take quite as much of the heat. He contacted the conference treasurer, a solid leader, to let him know and seek his counsel. The conference treasurer strongly recommended an outside audit, which the council reluctantly undertook. The council took some criticism from the people closest to the treasurer. The pastor knew they would have to work hard to rebuild trust in the congregation. Giving was down the next year, as they anticipated and planned for.

In a situation of financial wrongdoing, it is important to step back and take a wider view. The question in a crisis such as this is always, why now? A case of embezzlement or other financial wrongdoing is not just about the individual (a "bad apple"), but about the system as a whole. In this case, the growth in membership as well as the retirement of the previous pastor had unsettled the system. That pastor had been at the church for twenty years, an unusually long time for Methodist churches in general, and for this church in particular. This numerical and leadership shift upset the balance in the church. In fact, there was another instance of a financial meltdown that happened before the last pastor came—not embezzlement, but a serious budget crisis. In this church, money became a focus for the anxiety generated by transition in an extreme way.

The pastor appropriately triangled in the council president and, later, the conference treasurer. They both shared the responsibility for this problem. This is a case of a triangle being not necessarily negative, when a leader thoughtfully, not reactively, shares information with those who need to have it. Well-functioning leaders have ways to assess when to keep their own counsel and when to bring others in. When you suspect financial wrongdoing, it is important to bring in allies to handle the problem. This is no time to carry the load yourself.

Always focus on yourself and your own functioning first. In a crisis like this, it is easy to be flooded by anxiety, but you can remember this is not your problem alone; it is the church's problem as well. Ask, who are the key leaders who need to have the information as well as you? Mature leaders know when to step up and take responsibility; in this case, the minister knew he had to speak up. These leaders also know when to appropriately share the burden, and here again he knew this wasn't simply his to handle alone.

The treasurer was removed from his position, and his family left the church. People experienced grief at the loss, anger at the treasurer—and some were angry with the pastor for raising the issue. He did his best not to take it personally, and to move forward with his ministry. He recognized this might not be his most successful appointment, given the traumatic beginning, but he decided to work on loving the people, building and rebuilding relationships, and to see where it might go. He was exhausted when they got through it, and recognized he needed and wanted to pace himself and not expect too much of himself or others for a time. He simply paid attention to the basics for the next few months: getting to know people, being diligent in worship and preaching, tending to pastoral care, and managing some necessary administration.

◆ *Case 5. A building takes all the money*
In another situation, an Episcopal church finds itself with a building that sucks up a large portion of the budget, leaving little for program. The young rector begins to talk about the possibility of moving to a smaller building, more suited to their now-fewer membership. She has learned that a nearby church is for sale. The current wardens are open to the idea, but some of the vestry members are angry that the rector even raised the question.

In this denomination, decisions to sell one property and purchase another can be made by the vestry without approval from the membership, although these also must be approved by the diocesan standing committee and the bishop. Of course, without significant support of the members, the move will not succeed. Vestry members who are open raise both the question of timing and suitability: Do people have enough time to move through a process to make this decision? Is this property the right one? The rector has only been at the parish for two years, but has worked hard at establishing relationships with key members.

Formal and informal authority questions arise. In this church structure, the rector can make certain decisions alone, such as hiring and firing staff, unlike more congregational settings. But she cannot make the decision about the building without the support of others; she must persuade the vestry as well as diocesan leadership, and along with the vestry must persuade the congregation.

In a situation that is not a crisis, a decision like a move to save money needs to be done slowly. It might take a few years of holding conversations among all the stakeholders to come to a general agreement that this is the right decision—and of course there are some who will never agree. It is important not to allow a few naysayers to torpedo a necessary decision. Anxiety can cause leaders to make decisions too quickly or not quickly enough. Here the rector can be tempted to press for a decision, but it will probably damage her tenure, and may affect how those in the wider church view her leadership. Conversely, the vestry might never make a decision, until the parish's resources are exhausted and they only have enough money for a part-time rector, or must close entirely.

In this case, the leaders recognized they did not want to buy this property, but they began an honest conversation among themselves about how they were spending their money. The rector recognized she needed to slow down, while keeping the conversation open, especially with key leaders. She stayed in touch with the old guard—the altar guild and some key male leaders. They invited a diocesan staff person to help them moderate a few conversations, and that individual facilitated some helpful dialogue. Inviting a calm, neutral person to be present can be one way to create a useful triangle, whether that person is a denominational leader or an outside consultant.

Once the members opposed to the move saw that the rector was not trying to ram through a hasty action, they calmed down. In addition, the rector was calmer too, because she had stepped back from pressing the vestry to decide (an anxious stance) to a more open position ("I'd like us to keep talking about this and move toward making a decision one day"). Three years later, another property nearby became available, and the church, with diocesan assistance, was able to make the enormous decision to buy it and make a move.

IDEAS TO PONDER

As you face the inevitable money challenges in your own congregation, remember once again: money matters are always a focus for the anxiety, so just pay attention. Stay interested in how your congregation deals with money. It's possible to be a leader and a researcher at the same time—in fact, it can make for better leadership, because you will be calmer and more neutral. Don't take responsibility for the problems of others—even the church budget. The future of the church is up to the congregation and their ability to take responsibility for their life together.

◆ *Questions*
Here are seven questions to ask yourself about your own congregation to keep yourself thinking about money, authority, and emotional process.

1. How are decisions about money made in your church? Who is responsible?

2. What similarities can you see between how your church makes decisions about money and other decisions they make?

3. Who is the most anxious about money in your church? Who is the most calm?

4. Is there a place you need to define yourself about money ("Here's how I see it")?

5. Who are key people in the church you need to connect with?

6. What are the triangles related to money?

7. Who is overfunctioning around money? Are you? Who is underfunctioning? Are you?

chapter three

Lead in Stewardship

*The church budget is this: What is God calling us to do, and
what does it cost? That's the budget. God gives us all we have,
so all we're doing is giving back a small portion of that. In
thirty-four years of full-time ministry, every time I've taken the
risk to step out and say, we really need to do this because we
all know God is calling us, the money comes.*

— The Rev. Canon Howard Anderson, retired rector of
St. Matthew's Church in Pacific Palisades, California[1]

GENEROUS GIVING does not happen without leadership,
from both clergy and lay leaders. Leaders need to be clear about
their theology of stewardship, about their purpose and desire,
and about their roles. Clear and calm leadership is more important in the stewardship process than any fundraising technique.
Key elements include a fundamental theology of stewardship, a
clear vision for the congregation, and leaders who define themselves through every step of the stewardship process.

A THEOLOGICAL FOUNDATION
FOR STEWARDSHIP

To preach, teach, and lead in stewardship, you need to know
your own beliefs. It is important to take the time to think
through your own theology of stewardship in general and financial stewardship in particular. Here's one approach that is

grounded in a theology of abundance and trust in God, rather than anxiety about having enough.

Rooted in our understanding of creation, we celebrate all that is in our world and in our lives as a gift from God. We see the magnificence of nature, human relationships, and God's love for us. Out of the provision we have received, we give to God. Whether we have a lot or a little, our very breath comes as a gift. Therefore, we give not out of obligation, but out of gratitude.

All that we have is God's, not ours, so it's not a matter of "giving back" out of what is ours. Giving is a reminder that everything belongs to God anyway. The whole notion of stewardship is founded in this idea that we steward and care for and share God's world and God's resources. There is enough and more than enough. As Howard Anderson says, "We get very confused between God's economy and the world's economy. In the world's economy there's never enough, and when you're asking for money, you're taking something. In God's economy, there's always enough." God's relationship with creation itself is God's economy,[2] and that extends beyond anything we can imagine.

In addition to the spiritual value of knowing what we believe about stewardship, there is also a practical value. Understanding your own foundational beliefs will undergird your work in this area with greater energy and power. If you understand why you give and why you ask others to give, you can preach and teach on these matters with greater integrity, and with more energy and enthusiasm. You will be more present in your conversations about stewardship when you are not simply trying to raise funds for the church, but are speaking and acting out of your own deepest convictions. You will understand that you do not need to apologize for inviting people to give. Encouraging generosity and trust is one of the most important tasks of ministry, when we are able to make a genuine contribution toward helping people make the connection between their money and their faith so they can experience the intense joy giving can bring.

STEWARDSHIP AND VISION

Once you have some fundamental convictions clarified, the next step is to think about your vision for the ministry in the place where you serve. The job of the clergy leader is to see the bigger picture. It's essential for the pastor and other key leaders to know what the congregation is about and where it is headed. Additionally, you will have more energy for stewardship if you have some excitement about what the ministry is about, if you know what you are asking people to give to and why. Take some time to think it through. The vision doesn't have to be a huge one, just something you yourself can get excited about. Simply begin by asking yourself the question, what do you want for your church?

Over time, you can begin to develop a much longer-term view of the church's ministry. What do you want for your church in ten years, in thirty years, in one hundred years, long after you are gone? It is much easier to have an impact even in the short term if you begin to think with a perspective over time. We are part of the universal church which has been around for two thousand years and talks about a future which includes eternity. Yet most churches do not think about more than one year at a time. One idea is for church leaders to develop a specific, long-term budget for their organizations, as a way to communicate what could lie ahead. Specific numbers allow leaders to be specific in the ways that they might reach those numbers. A long-term budget is one way to think about vision. It's hard work to put together such a budget—it forces you to think about what you want, so that you are able to say, "This is not a prediction, it's a direction." This could create a remarkable conversation between clergy and lay leadership about where they want to go together. I believe the pastoral leader carries the responsibility for starting the conversation by sharing what he or she wants for the ministry, both now and in the future.

Of course the vision requires more than one person to articulate and support it, even when that person is the pastor. The vision is not all about you, though your leadership is important. Robert L. Hunter, a congregational consultant and long-time director of stewardship at Second Presbyterian Church in Indianapolis, suggests, "By vision I don't mean the pastor's dream or the treasurer's sacred cow. I mean a broadly held vision within the congregation of what they want to be and want to accomplish." This kind of broad vision does not emerge overnight, yet finding your own clarity and beginning a conversation with key leaders about purpose and direction is an essential part of the ministry of stewardship, as well as the overall ministry of the church. It's critical to encouraging people to give with generosity. Hunter adds, "Increasingly, fundraising even within the church is going to have to answer the question, 'Why should I give to you rather than someone else?'"[3]

If the pastor has at least begun to articulate a clear vision and is present in his or her leadership role, it will be much easier to generate enough funds to support the ministry. People will not give just because they ought to—they need to know what they are giving to and why they are giving it. Current research shows the most important reason people give to the church is a belief in its mission.

The second reason people give is having a regard for staff leadership.[4] People need and want to know what they are giving for, and they need to know the leader is present and accounted for. In their remarkable study of stewardship, *Passing the Plate,* Christian Smith, Michael Emerson, and Patricia Snell observed two categories for how clergy tend to lead around money: "Pay the bills" and "Live the vision," with a spectrum between the two. They discovered, not surprisingly, that leaders who live a vision are able to encourage people to give more.[5]

In boom times or in difficult times, articulating a vision is very different from asking the question, "How do we get them to give more?" Rather, it is asking the question, "What do we want to do together?" and enlisting others to support that endeavor. Bob Hunter challenges pastors to develop a case statement in the traditional philanthropic sense—a compelling case for support that grows out of the vision of this congregation. This statement clearly outlines the purpose, program, and financial needs of the ministry. A critical portion of the role responsibility of a pastor is to be the key spokesperson, from the pulpit and elsewhere, to make this case for the ministry of the church.

STEWARDSHIP PREACHING

It takes more than one good sermon to undergird the steward-ship ministry of your congregation. Church leaders can put a lot of weight on that sermon or sermon series, but stewardship preaching and teaching must take place in the context of the overall vision and direction of the congregation, as well as within any particular program you may implement. That said, preaching remains a critical part of any stewardship endeavor. In almost all churches, worship remains the time when you have the greatest critical mass of members and friends. The sermon, even in more liturgical churches, is a central part of worship. Attending to the important task of preaching on the topic of giv-ing is worth the effort.

There is a tension in all preaching, and especially preaching about stewardship, when you are acknowledging that you want more for people in their relationship with money and with giv-ing, while also letting go of the intense desire to change other people. Paradoxically, the more you try to use preaching to change people, the less they are likely to be changed. The more you say, in essence, "You should give more," or, "You should be less materialistic," the more they resist. The more frustrated you are, the less effective your preaching will be.

Instead, work to offer your preaching in a spirit of openness to people as they are in the way they relate to money and to stewardship. The most powerful preaching about giving comes from a place of self-definition: "Here's what I believe about giv-ing." "This is how I understand the Scriptures and God's call on our lives." "Here is what I want for our church." "Here is what I want for myself in my relationship with money." You can say, "Here is what I'd like." Don't hesitate to ask people to give, but do it from an emotional space of openness.

Tips for Preaching about Stewardship and Money

1

Define your own views in your stewardship sermons. See them
as opportunities for the congregation to hear what you think,
rather than occasions to convince them to do something.

2

Acknowledge to the congregation your own challenges in this area.
Stand alongside them, rather than over them, pointing a finger.

3

Talk about your own efforts to relate spirituality and money. You don't
have to reveal your deepest secrets about your financial life, but you can
share something of yourself as a way to help others grow.

4

Preach a sermon at a time that is not stewardship / pledge time, in
which you articulate your values about money to the congregation.

5

Tell stories in your sermons about the church's money past, especially
its founding. Be honest about past financial challenges, but remember
to include stories about the strengths and successes, too.

6

When you are preaching at stewardship time, don't hesitate to ask
people openly to support the ministry of the church.
There's no need to be apologetic about giving.

The pulpit is not the only place where clergy have the opportunity to influence people in relation to their giving. Bible studies and adult education classes are also places to consider how you might influence others. Vestry/council and committee meetings are ready-made places to do a few minutes of teaching, and board retreats are also places to talk about giving. Tell your own story, and invite others to tell theirs. Share with them what you want for them in regard to stewardship and their relationship with money. Then, ask them what *they* want. The benefit of these more informal settings is the opportunity for give-and-take. These sessions may actually have the potential for *more* impact on the individuals who attend, because they can be more engaged in their own thinking and learning.

I recommend in any setting, whether it's a class or a brief learning time in a meeting, to present a few thoughts, then give people time to think for themselves and jot down a few of their own ideas. You might even try this in a sermon. This helps develop self-directed learning and is more likely to produce results over time. Invite them to make a commitment to themselves, even a small one. For example, someone might declare they intend to reflect on where they learned about giving. Or they might figure out what percentage of their income they give. You don't have to have all the ideas; rather, you can invite them to reflect thoughtfully on their relationship to money.

You can find a number of valuable resources to use for educating key leaders. Check out the Ecumenical Stewardship Center, www.stewardshipresources.org, for example. See especially their digital resource *Teaching a Christian View of Money: Celebrating God's Generosity* by Barbara J. Fullerton and Mark L. Vincent. Charles R. Lane's book, *Ask, Thank, Tell: Improving Stewardship Ministry in Your Congregation,* would be an excellent study book for a board or stewardship committee.

Won't people get tired of all this talk about money? You may not want to do it at every council retreat or every adult education session. But over time a periodic focus on how people relate to money can be of real benefit to them in their daily lives. You may find they thank you.

SELF-DEFINITION AND GIVING

In all your preaching and teaching about stewardship and money, remember to clearly define yourself. Keep a perspective on where you end and other people begin. Allow others to make their own choices about giving, while clearly stating your own position. As you state your beliefs about giving, you invite others to think through their own giving and make a commitment. You respect their power over their own life and resources, and they will sense this automatically.

Why is self-definition so important? Isn't the point of stewardship preaching and teaching to get people to give more, to change their relationship with money, to support the ministry better? Stewardship education at its best is an invitation to a new relationship to God and to our resources. I liken it to evangelism—the most powerful evangelism involves telling your own story and inviting people toward the possibility of faith. People resist and resent being willed. Anxious preaching about money quickly becomes willful and has less impact than a clear telling of our own relationship with money, coupled with an invitation that is freely offered, allowing people to make their own choices.

One pastor had led his church through some exciting times, including significant community outreach and a new building. After fifteen years, he was dreading this year's stewardship campaign. Over the years, he had been given and had taken on too much responsibility for raising the money. He had been convincing and cajoling people to support the budget and special projects for most of those years. By accepting too much responsibility for raising the money, he was allowing other leaders and the rest of the congregation to avoid their own responsibility. He recognized the imbalance of appropriate responsibility among the rest of the congregation, and decided that he needed to make a shift in his own functioning. So he told the council president he was going to take a new approach this year. When the change was shared with the members of the council, they were a little unsure, but because he had been pastor long enough and had been successful they believed him despite their doubts. From the pulpit, the pastor spoke candidly to the congregation: "Here is what we're hoping can happen in this congregation, and here is why I'm asking you to support it." He made a very specific case for increasing their giving in the congregation. Then he said, "I'm not going to tell you what you ought to do. I am asking you to prayerfully consider your pledge this year, and respond accordingly." A few members were disgruntled. Yet to his surprise as much as everyone else's, pledges were up 20 percent in that campaign. And giving followed suit.

TELL YOUR OWN STORY

Early in my own ministry, I always found stewardship season anxiety-producing. While I got better at it, I still found the fall campaign difficult. One year the program we were using strongly suggested the pastor make his or her pledge public as part of the stewardship sermon. In our congregation there was a lot of anxiety about the confidentiality of giving records. But I realized that no one could say I couldn't reveal my own secret. At the end of my sermon, I got out my pledge card. I said, "My pledge this year will be X dollars," and I filled it in right at the pulpit. People gasped. As someone who tithed, I was one of the bigger givers in the church—and no one knew it. One woman told me later she crossed out the number on her card and filled in a larger one. Pledges did go up significantly that year. And more important, it got me freer about money. I had defined myself, in public, to them, about something that was very important to me. One secret had been told. I continued to talk about my own giving every year as long as I was there, and giving continued to go up. I felt much less anxious about the entire process from that time forward.

Testifying is one of the best ways to lead. It is self-definition. Telling your own story is far more powerful than the leader telling others what they should do. This approach is more than a stewardship technique. It is a way to show up more present in this process of speaking to others about giving. You don't have to be a perfect example for your story to have power for others. Joe Clifford of First Presbyterian Church of Dallas tells about sharing his own giving story in a stewardship-oriented sermon:

> I talked about a time in my life when I was giving $500 to the church. I felt like I was doing pretty well: I'd never given $500 a year to anything in my life. But I realized I was giving 1 percent of what I was earning, and that really wasn't a big deal. We got on the journey toward tithing. We couldn't start at 10 percent but we started at 2 percent and we worked our way up, and over time we got to 10 percent. I was very honest about the fact that we set a personal goal to be at a tithe, but there are years we make it and years we don't. I had so many people who came to me and said, "Thank you so much for being that honest."[6]

People respect candid leadership, especially around something as challenging as making giving decisions.

Consider sharing some of your own family story as part of stewardship sermons. Another Presbyterian pastor, Jonathan Eric Carroll, suggests that it can be enlightening for others to hear the preacher reflect on his or her own family. You might share how your family handled issues of money and stewardship, and who you are becoming in light of those family dynamics, in addition to reflecting on the biblical text.[7]

Of course, telling the story is not simply up to the top leader. It's important to share this responsibility, too. Other key lay leaders must be involved and willing to say boldly, "Here's what I think is important about our church and about giving and why." Clergy can coach lay leaders to define *themselves* around why they give to the church, to tell their own story in a compelling way. The best stewardship testimonies can make the sermon that Sunday seem almost unnecessary. When clergy and lay leaders are in partnership, and are all able to share clearly why they give to the church, it creates a powerful message to the congregation.

LEADING WITHOUT OVERFUNCTIONING OR UNDERFUNCTIONING

How can you engage more fully in the stewardship process, without overfunctioning or underfunctioning? The functioning of the leader is more important than any stewardship program.

Some programs may be better than others, yet any program can work if the leader is present and accounted for, has a solid relationship with the congregation, and defines him or herself around vision and around giving. The congregation inevitably looks to the pastor for leadership. And the best program can fail if the leader doesn't show up. The people sense the minister's discomfort or hesitancy, and will hold back themselves. If the pastor is afraid to talk about money or ask people to give in a straightforward way, any stewardship effort will have reduced impact. And a pastor who overcomes that fear and talks with courage about giving and finances can have a profound influence on giving over time. Even those who initially bristle at a greater emphasis on giving can come around when the clergy leader stays clear and calm on the subject.

Be clear on what you are responsible for and what you are not responsible for. In the stewardship process, clergy often underperform in vision and leadership, and overperform in administrative tasks. As I have noted, the pastor needs to have a public role in making the case for giving. In addition, to lead stewardship you need key allies, appropriate connections, and other people to help carry the load. The pastor needs to manage his or her tendency to take too much responsibility in relation to the nuts-and-bolts work of the stewardship committee or team. Stay connected to that group, but don't do their work for them. In smaller churches in particular, this can be tempting. Resist taking over. James Lamkin, pastor of Northside Drive Baptist Church in Atlanta, puts it this way: "I try to think overtly before we begin the stewardship campaign about what is my role in this system. For instance, if I'm sitting in on a finance committee meeting, what is my role in this meeting? I'm not on the finance committee; I'm not the chair." One year, when he had the opportunity to review the stewardship letter, he noticed that there were no references to God or Jesus, and suggested that in a letter going out to a Baptist congregation that might be important to include. He offered appropriate input based on his role.[8]

Ask yourself, what is appropriate functioning and what is overfunctioning as a leader? It's not always easy to tell. Be clear what it means to be the pastoral leader of *your* church's stewardship program. What role functions are important? What is yours to carry, and what do you need to share with others? And what does appropriate functioning mean for the lay leaders? What do they need to do in their roles? Asking these questions when planning for stewardship will lead to different choices than if we plunge ahead and take charge without thinking about it (overfunctioning), or simply abdicate leadership to others (underfunctioning).

Clergy can delegate many aspects of stewardship, and should. But you cannot delegate the role of chief spokesperson for the importance and value of giving. If you are the pastor, priest, or rector, no one else can fill that role. It's simply part of the pastoral job description. If you find this a challenge, as Eleanor Roosevelt said, "You must do the thing you think you cannot do." In addition, if you take it on, you'll get better at it. The more you talk about money, the more comfortable you will be talking about it.

Lay leaders also share the responsibility to function well and to stay relatively calm. Even if there's a budget shortfall, a spirit of calm and a sense of possibility among all the key leaders make it more likely that the congregation will meet the challenge. One church faced the retirement of a long-term minister and realized they had been significantly underpaying him. As the interim period began, the lay leaders were anxious about how church members would respond when they realized they would have to increase their compensation package considerably to attract a new minister. But they calmed down, clarified their own understanding of what was needed, and challenged the church members to increase their giving. Lay leadership is an essential part of developing stewardship throughout the life cycle of a congregation.

STEWARDSHIP AND THE PASTOR'S SALARY

What do pastors do with the fact that, after all, the giving supports *them*? Many clergy name this as one of the big challenges in stewardship. They feel uncomfortable about the fact that their compensation may be 50 percent of the budget in a smaller congregation. I believe this is an exercise in maturity: to remain convinced of the value not only of the ministry of the church, but of your own work, and to confidently and unapologetically ask others to support that work. Indeed, if you are the minister, you are paid that salary to be the leader. And if you are not leading in this area of money, then people will be less willing to support the ministry of the church. Believe it or not, they need you to ask them to give. In the words of Scripture, "You do not have because you do not ask" (James 4:2). If you do ask clearly and without hesitation, giving will be stronger.

Pat, a new pastor in a smaller UCC congregation, was about to give her first stewardship sermon, and she was feeling anxious about it. So she called her mentor, and asked, "How can I ask them to give when half of what they give goes to pay me?" Her mentor coached her to remember the worth of her work, and to speak calmly and without being defensive about her own view of the church's future ministry, what she thought about giving, and why she herself gave to the church. Standing in the pulpit, she looked out at the congregation, and realized how much she looked forward to what they could do together with more resources. When you keep your focus on the ministry, you will find it easier to boldly preach stewardship.

HOW MUCH TO GIVE

I advocate the tithe. I want more people to be tithers, to give at least 10 percent of their income. Given how wealthy we are, considered globally and historically, it is a guideline that continues to be relevant. I do not believe it is a legalistic requirement. I believe that people who tithe do not regret it. For those who do not yet tithe, considering giving as a percentage of income is a way to increase it incrementally, with the tithe as a goal. Teaching tithing is a way to challenge people to give more, in a clear, defined way. We can use teaching about the tithe not as a weapon but as an invitation, to help people arrange the priorities in their lives. Remember that many people did not grow up learning about tithing or even giving. Have some structured way to teach newcomers and young people about the theology and practice of giving, and about the meaning of tithing. Don't assume that people know already. Even some people who grow up in church with parents who give never receive any instruction about giving, let alone tithing.

In addition, how much the clergy leader gives, as a percentage of income, is important. Clergy may face many life circumstances which make tithing a challenge, but it will strengthen your preaching and teaching about money if you are giving generously yourself. This may not apply to everything, but it applies to giving. It's hard to convincingly ask people to consider tithing if you are not tithing, or moving toward tithing. I believe it's best if pastors give 10 percent, and are encouraging lay leaders and church members to do so, too. You do not have to be apologetic about offering the challenge. Just keep talking about it, inviting people to tithe and to say publicly that they tithe. Recruit stewardship speakers who are tithers, or who are committed to incrementally increasing their giving as a percentage of income.

Additionally, it is also important that key leaders be generous givers. Howard Anderson insists that all the members of his vestry be tithers. Most clergy are not that bold. Still, I do think that having people in key leadership positions who are not giving well automatically limits what you are able to do financially and in other ways in ministry. Leaders need to have some way to assess the giving of those who are in key positions.

WHO KNOWS WHO GIVES

Should clergy know how much people give? Churches are different and pastors are different. That is why I do not think there's a right answer to this question, although I am inclined to suggest you move toward the pastor knowing about giving. I would put it this way: if the reason you do not know who gives is that the least mature are calling the shots, that's a problem. One argument for pastors knowing who gives what is that you do not want key leaders to be people who are giving little or nothing. When the pastor does not have giving information, he or she is on the outside of a key triangle in church life, and I think that's a problem. The financial secretary or whoever keeps the records knows more than the pastor. Howard Anderson has strong opinions about this subject: "It's absolutely essential. You are irresponsible not to know." There are pastoral issues at stake, not just financial. Anderson suggests that if someone suddenly stops giving, you need to call on them, because something is wrong. They may have lost their job or be facing a marital crisis, or they might be angry with you about something. "One of the best spiritual indicators is people's giving patterns, so you need to know not only how much they give," Anderson believes, but you also need to have some way to know when people's giving has fallen off or increased dramatically.[9]

All this said, it can be challenging to make a change like this in churches where the tradition of the pastor not knowing is very strong, as is the case in many Baptist churches. Over time, it is important to pick your battles, as experienced clergy know. One Baptist pastor put it out before he was called: "If you call me to be the pastor, I will know the giving records."

FACING RESISTANCE

If leaders decide to move forward in a new direction with a clear, focused stewardship emphasis, chances are some resistance will emerge. How do you handle objections to more intentional stewardship teaching? Remember, the people who object the loudest are often giving the least. (This is another argument for the pastor knowing who gives what, so you know what weight to give to these objections.) Friedman called dealing with intense resistance, which he described as sabotage, "the keys to the kingdom" in leadership. It is critical not to be derailed by the naysayers; it is equally essential to have key allies in lay leadership. You cannot make this shift alone. Don't get defensive, and don't try to argue people into submission. Instead, work hard to stay calm, to be relatively light about it, and to stay on track with your plans. You can frame the new approach as an experiment (recognizing that this will not derail the most vociferous and noisy objectors). Simply have the courage of your convictions, and coach lay leaders to do the same. Of course, in some churches these objections can become extremely intense. One pastor found that two key leaders threatened to withdraw their large pledges when he led the church to offer a challenging stewardship campaign. He stuck to his guns, the leaders did hold back their pledges—and the church still met its goal. It wasn't easy, but it was an act of leadership that will have benefits far beyond the church budget When leaders can stand up to those who try to hold the congregation hostage to their own giving, the whole community is better off.

Resistance may also show up in other areas besides threats to reduce giving: for instance, criticism of the pastor's performance in areas that have nothing to do with money—staff issues, perhaps, or grumbling about board leadership. A systems view of congregations recognizes that all aspects of our life together are connected. It's like a mobile: move one piece, and the whole mobile bounces. Tampering with long-held approaches to stewardship can upset the balance in the congregation. How accurately can you predict where your church might react? While you may need to address the issues raised, when you keep the perspective of the mobile, you will know not to take the criticisms or other upsets too seriously. If you stay calm, the mobile will rebalance.

CHANGING ATTITUDES TO GIVING

Leaders need to continue to develop and adapt their approach to stewardship. It's no secret that times are changing. Overall giving patterns are changing, and were in flux long before the 2008 crisis. Giving as a percentage of income has been in decline for decades. In 2009 it was 2.38 percent of Protestant per-member income, the lowest level in forty-one years.[10] Overall giving dollars are declining as well: charitable giving to religion decreased by 8.1 percent (inflation-adjusted) from 2009 to 2011.[11] In addition, competition for charitable dollars has increased dramatically. Fifty-five percent of all charitable dollars used to go to the church; today it is 33 percent.[12] As a result, it is even more critical to clearly articulate the vision and to ask people to support it. Other organizations are doing so, and people—many of them members of local churches—are responding. Increasingly, people give to specific projects rather than general budgets. Besides a well-articulated vision and a well-run overall stewardship campaign, we can also develop specific projects, and ask people to support those. Second Presbyterian Church in Indianapolis has worked to encourage younger members to give now to specific endowed projects, not by estate planning. There are many ways to be inventive as we encourage people of all generations to give.[13]

Of course, we have seen rapidly evolving financial circumstances through the economic upheaval in recent years—both churches and families are struggling. We have to be creative about inviting people to give when we all are even more anxious than usual about money, and when we know that people in our congregation have lost jobs. Here are three ways to approach stewardship in challenging times.

First, *be honest about the external situation and the church's budget situation*. Facts are helpful. Even difficult facts, calmly presented by leadership with the message, "We can handle this," help calm people down. For instance, one Episcopal church in the New York area faced a major budget challenge in 2009 due to a huge loss in endowment income, plus the loss of giving from families in the financial services industry. The financial crisis had a profound impact on the wider community and the church's ministry, and on many families within the church. The rector and vestry chairperson initially addressed the parish membership, both saying, "We don't know exactly what's going to happen, but we're sure we can get through this. We're going to help and encourage the families that are affected, and we are committed to finding the best way to continue our ministry in this place." Their calm demeanor helped others stay calm.

Second, *give people some breathing room,* so they can calm down and think through their questions: What can I afford to do this year? What am I called to do now and in the future? Give them freedom to say, "my situation is different now," without guilt. For some families growing in giving may mean giving less in a given year, if they are facing different circumstances. When people feel accepted no matter what they are able to give, they are less likely to distance from the community and more likely to increase their giving again when they are later able to do so.

Finally, *don't hesitate to challenge those who are able to give generously* as a response to God, and to help the church through a difficult period. We offer the opportunity for them to grow spiritually in relation to their money. Don't assume that everyone will need to reduce their giving. Even in an economic downturn some will continue to have plenty of resources.

The stakes can seem very high in today's challenging economy. Yet you will be better off the more you can hold the task lightly, and see how people respond to an honest acknowledgment of the facts, coupled with a sense of possibility and hope. Keep your wits about you, and encourage other leaders to do the same. We will all need to remain light on our feet as we face a changing generational and economic environment in the years and decades to come.[14]

HELPING PEOPLE RELATE TO MONEY ALL YEAR LONG

Stewardship is about far more than preaching about money one or two Sundays a year. It is not simply about supporting the budget. Rather, it is a ministry to help people learn about their relationship to money, and to other ways they can give. This chapter focuses on encouraging financial giving to the ministry of the church, of course. Yet overall financial education—helping people grow in their relationship to their own personal finances—can be a vital part of stewardship. People will find it hard to make decisions about giving if their own financial house is not in order. Conversely, when they feel more clarity and control over their own relationship with their resources, they will find it easier to say yes to more giving.

So it is important to talk about money and faith frequently: from the pulpit, in educational settings, and in pastoral care. This is a profound pastoral need in churches. People touch money every day of their lives, and they desperately need help. Israel Galindo, Associate Dean for Lifelong Learning at Columbia Theological Seminary, says that all too often we give people no help during the year to deal with what money represents in their lives from a faith perspective. He says, "Then once a year we ask them for more money while they are dealing with all this anxiety about money. So if part of my pastoral responsibility is the spiritual welfare of my congregation, I cannot avoid dealing with this real, critical faith issue in the life of my members. It's not about the budget; it's about a Christian response to the resources you have."[15] Expanding your understanding of your ministry in this area beyond simply supporting the budget or even the vision will be a huge contribution to your people.

For many clergy, this means overcoming the tendency to avoid financial issues and to be relieved when stewardship season is over. As I said, early in my ministry I dreaded the fall campaign and was glad when it was completed. Yet over time I learned to view it as an opportunity for ministry, to support people as they grew in their spiritual and financial lives. We developed a year-round stewardship focus rather than limiting it to a few weeks in the fall. This shift took the pressure off the "campaign" season, and enabled us to provide other opportunities for learning, such as a financial education program.

As you engage in the long-term education of your members regarding faith and finances, remember that people change slowly over something as fraught as money. Think five years, or more. Then you and your leaders can look back and see what has happened, and celebrate the results. Think about what you want for people in terms of their relationship with their resources. Write it down for yourself: "I want the majority of people in this congregation to be tithers." "I want the people of this church to give out of love and not out of duty." "I want the people of this community to see their daily relationship with money from a spiritual perspective." When you are clear on what you want for your people, you can make choices about how to preach and teach to offer them a path to get there. You can tell them what you want, and why: "I want you to see your money as a gift from God, because I believe there is greater freedom when you see money from a spiritual perspective." This approach to teaching and preaching about finances is far different from willing others to be different. It gives people room to do their own thinking: "What do I think about what the pastor says he wants?" "How am I going to respond to what she said today?" "What do *I* want from my relationship with my re-sources?" When people begin to do their own reflecting on their life with money, change will happen.

CELEBRATING THE PRIVILEGE OF THE MINISTRY OF STEWARDSHIP

We can find much to enjoy and even celebrate about the stew-ardship process, rather than dreading it or viewing it as a neces-sary evil. We get to talk about money, which most of us badly need to get better at. We have the chance to articulate something important about the vision and ministry of our church. We have the privilege of getting people involved in giving, some for the very first time. Make your own list about what you can celebrate about the need to raise money for your church's ministry.

It is possible to enjoy stewardship season more. Here are sev-eral ways to do so.

1. Think about the stewardship process as ministry, not as a tedious chore that you have to get through. You'll enjoy it more.

2. Enter into it as a learner. See what you can learn about your congregation, as well as new developments in stewardship. Read one book about stewardship every year. Find a stewardship blog or other online resource that you like and check it frequently.

3. Imagine together ways you can make it fun. Invite more fun people to be on the committee. Collect humor about stewardship and about money. Do what you can to get yourself a little lighter. Invite a young person to be part of the stewardship process. Develop your own ideas to frame stewardship as ministry, to keep learning about stewardship and to make it more fun.

4. Celebrate those who give to your church. Having generous givers, whether they give a lot or a little, during their lifetime or after their death, makes a difference in the life of a congregation. We often do little to

acknowledge those who give. It could be fun for everyone to do more celebrating. Giving may increase—but even better, leaders can feel lighter about the stewardship enterprise. When pastors and church leaders put a positive focus all year long on all those who give, the whole church can benefit.

Tips for Celebrating Those Who Give

1

Write a thank you note by hand to each giver of record. In today's world, a handwritten note will make a powerful impression.

2

Celebrate in worship those who give,
outside of stewardship season.

3

When you highlight a ministry in worship, in a publication,
or on your website, make a point about those who support
it by giving their time and money.

4

Use social media to thank those who give.
(If you don't know how, ask a young person.
If you do know how, teach other people who need to know.)

5

Tell the story of someone who left a legacy to the church,
recently or long ago.

6

Celebrate the founding members of your church.
If any are still living, thank them in person.

7

For pastors, preach a sermon celebrating those who give,
without asking people to give.

8

Celebrate and thank those who give
sacrificially on a small income.

9

When you receive the final total in pledges,
have a big celebration in worship and after worship.

10

Ask an artist in your congregation to create something
beautiful to celebrate your givers.

IDEAS TO PONDER

Whether it's campaign season or not, keep asking yourself questions that will lead to greater clarity about stewardship and will help you get some distance from the understandable anxiety about next year's budget. Step back from your own anxiety about staffing, your salary, and the uncertain economy. Figure out what *you* think. Then, think about what you want to say to the church about what you think. It can help others to know what *they* think, if you acknowledge the complexity of these matters, and that you struggle, too.

◆ *Questions*

Here are four questions to ask yourself as you continue to do the important ongoing work of clarifying your personal thinking about stewardship.

1. Why do you give? For most of us, there is a variety of reasons: our values, our upbringing, our position of

leadership, a sense of obligation, love. See if you can untangle some of these threads for yourself.

2. What did you learn about giving from your family of origin? I can remember getting a one-dollar allowance and being expected to give a dime. As a young adult, the first time I chose not to tithe it made me very anxious—I was breaking the family rules. Over time, I had to figure out what I myself thought about those rules, and chose to tithe for myself. What do you think about your family rules about giving?

3. Why do you give the amount you give? Do you tithe? Why? Do you and your spouse or partner agree on these matters? How do you make the decisions you do?

4. Why do you give where you give? Do you give most of your tithe or other charitable giving to the church, or do you divide it up? Why? How do you respond to those phone calls? Do you give to everyone who comes along, or not? Why?

chapter four

Explore Your Church's Financial Past

*I do believe that the past plays an important, often
unarticulated role in creating the present-day realities of
religious institutions. Memories survive in different
ways, sometimes as a deep undercurrent of sadness or
disappointment, sometimes as a tendency toward suspicion
of outsiders or as resentment of authority. The past can work
in positive ways too, inuring a centuries-old congregation
against panic or despair. All this suggests the importance of
understanding the institutional DNA of a place—that broad
set of predilections that shape (but do not determine) a
church or a denomination's life course.*

— Margaret Bendroth, "The Past Isn't Past"[1]

PHILIP, A UCC MINISTER, was visiting the oldest
member of his church. Mary had grown up in the church, and
her parents were founding members. He asked Mary what her
parents said about Reverend Stone, the first minister. She replied
that everyone said he kept the church afloat: "He shook people
upside down to empty their pockets so the church could stay
open." Philip realized that the council expected him to shake
people upside down, too—and he had happily done so. He
hadn't quite realized it, and he certainly hadn't known this was
a congregational tradition.

KNOW YOUR CHURCH'S MONEY STORY

Do you wonder why your church does what it does around money? It's easy to celebrate or blame individuals in church life—the generous giver, the difficult treasurer. Yet money patterns are not simply about key people. Rather, these behaviors may be part of the church's heritage. Past patterns in relating to money frequently persist. Some churches have a long history of conflict over money; others pass the budget every year without a ripple. Some churches are generous with staff; others begrudge every nickel in increases, year after year, decade after decade. Some churches generously support community outreach, generation after generation; other congregations never believe they have enough, despite a large endowment. When you visit a church, you instantly have a sense of its personality the minute you walk in the door. That personality goes beyond the surface, deep into the life of the church. When it comes to money, what do you see in your church: generosity or stinginess, outward focus or inward focus, careful planning or crisis mentality?

When you are dealing with money at church, the past is always present, and it's important to pay attention to it. Making sense of the past can help you lead in the present. Of course, you do not want to be mired in the past. At the same time, you do not want to ignore it, because it can trip you up. Understanding your church's money history can explain sometimes puzzling patterns, and give perspective on why changing them is so difficult. It can also help you see unexpected strengths that can help you all work together for a better future.

The founding story of your church is one critical way the past is present. If your church started with the enthusiastic financial support of its first members, chances are you still have members enthusiastically supporting the church's ministry. If you received substantial funding from your denomination at the beginning, your church might have an entitlement mentality—or a confidence that the bottom line will always be met. If your church began in an acrimonious split from another church about money, there will be some residue in relation to finance, whether it happened last year or two generations ago. The earliest patterns of relationship in churches frequently persist over time.

Moreover, money-related issues that emerge throughout the lifetime of the church also can have an impact on the future. A series of successful capital fund drives makes the success of campaigns in the future more likely. If there was a fight over property or money, look for that to show up in your church's financial life over time. A formerly German-speaking church discovered old board minutes, in German, detailing the fight the board had about whether to build a one-seat or a two-seat outhouse. Some did not want to spend the money for the two-seater. Today the penny-pinching emerges in not wanting to spend money on an updated website. Beliefs about history also influence the present: the stories people believe are true have power even if they are only partially true ("This place was rolling with money in the fifties").

Emotional intensity around money gets passed down from generation to generation, in churches as well as families. You might wonder, if these behaviors are transmitted, *how* does it happen? It makes sense this might happen in families, but how does it take place in institutions, where people are not even related? There are no easy answers for this—sometimes it seems almost mysterious. Why *is* it that one family always gives the lion's share of the budget, for example? Over the years, it's not even the same family, but the pattern persists.

There are some logical elements at work here. Early in a church's story relationship patterns are developed. The pastors who come to serve that church and the people who join it fit the mold, with its strengths and weaknesses. The whole becomes larger than the sum of its parts, and the patterns persist. Pastors and lay leaders come in and try to change the culture, to encourage others to give more, or to fight less about money. Yet once the form has taken place, it's not so easy to change. After twenty-five or fifty or one hundred years, it takes more than a year to shift these behaviors.

What can church leaders do about these realities? Instead of tearing your hair out, do a little research and learn more about your church's past. Make friends with the church historian and read past annual reports: you may be surprised by what you learn. One pastor read through years of reports for the church he served and noticed every single pastor tried to convince people to support the church better financially, going back before he was born. He realized the chance of him making a significant shift in those patterns, as he had hoped to do when he arrived, was small. In a way, this long-term perspective takes the pressure off. Keeping an eye on the sweep of congregational history reminds ministers that their time with these people is brief, relatively speaking. And it helps avoid the Messiah-complex that can be so tempting to clergy. If your parish has a long history, dig through the layers to see what you can find out. You do not have to read every ledger, but read some key reports, and ask key leaders for their stories. Even if your church is young, there is financial history that you need to learn. As I have noted, pay particular attention to the founding story. If you are the founding pastor, it still pays to think about the dynamics that went into funding your church, and the patterns you are creating that can affect future generations.

When clergy first start at a church, they have a great excuse to ask questions about finances. Organizational consultant Kathy Wiseman suggests that you work hard first thing to relate to whoever is responsible for financial decision-making, both paid and unpaid. Get to know them, and ask them about each turning point in the financial history—what was it, how did they get to it, and how did they get out of it? Then ask, "Who else should I talk to? Because financial responsibility is on the top of my list for a high-functioning organization." This strategy accomplishes a couple of important tasks: it helps you develop relationships with the key money players first thing, and it gives you information you need to assess the system of which you have become a part.[2]

However, you do not have to be new in your congregation to benefit from this research. It's never too late to start. You can begin to put together the pieces of the story you already know into a coherent whole, understanding more deeply the forces that have made your congregation what it is, and how finances are a part of that. As you track the history, see if you can connect financial happenings with other events in the life of the church, in the community, or in your denomination. Any church is part of a larger system. If your church existed during the Great Depression, or a more recent economic downturn, how did it weather that? Can you find out? You may find resilience you did not expect. If your church has a significant anniversary coming up, it's a good opportunity for you to learn more. If there are anniversary histories, read them with new eyes, looking for clues to their story with money, at the beginning and through the years. The point of the research is not to accumulate information for yet another "History of First Church" document. Rather, it is to support you in your leadership, to deepen your understanding of your people, and to help you be less reactive and more thoughtful about the ministry and financial decisions that need to be made in the present.

It can take years to get the whole story. Still, leaders who listen for the stories over time can learn a lot about how their church functions now. Knowing the past does not necessarily mean we can change the patterns, yet when we know more, we can be more neutral about the sometimes surprising decisions about money that congregations make.

One Episcopal priest had a wealthy church member tell him, "This should be a poor church." He learned that the church had for decades approached ministry funding by talking up the desperate need for funds in the short term rather than charting a ministry direction. When a money crunch came, the previous rector was expected to drive around and request money from wealthy families. Also, the families of wealth in the congregation did not want to appear too generous lest it inhibit other givers. The current rector learned about this practice when the business manager told him, "By the way, you should know we have $37 in the operating account." She expected he would follow the pattern. Instead he said, "That is not going to happen."

This rector took some time to reflect on what he had learned, and then called a parish meeting for the following Sunday to pass along the information about the $37, asking them the question, "What do you think we should do about this situation?" The parish had been consistently sheltered from knowing anything about the financial life of the parish. He began to insist that they talk together about their ministry and to ask questions about what was the best way to fund it consistently, rather than lurching from crisis to crisis. Several years later, he finds there is still resistance to transparency about money. What you learn becomes a reality check: if this church has had a mid-year financial crisis for forty years, you are not going to worry so much about this year's crunch since the parish always seems to come through by the end of the year. And you can then make choices about how to speak with leaders and members about finances that are grounded in their own history, even as you challenge them to function in new ways.

You can be more creative in your approach to leadership around stewardship and finance, and be less frustrated overall, if you recognize the power of past patterns. You will have a better sense of what you are facing, and the kind of patience and persistence that will be required to make a difference in the long term. A Baptist pastor discovered as she began to look into the story of her own church that the lay leadership liked to keep the pastor on the outside of financial decision-making. At first she had thought it was because she was a woman. Yet when she talked to her predecessor, she learned they did the same thing to him. And about a year into her pastorate she found an old letter from a pastor a generation before, suggesting that the same thing was true.

So she realized this was not anything personal, and she didn't make an issue of it. She had to deal with her own feelings of being excluded, but she remembered the history and worked hard not to take it personally. She kept showing up at the trustees' meetings, and she always learned something about the church at the meetings. She also learned to show up occasionally at the café where several of them gathered for coffee every Wednesday. They still forgot to notify her of the meetings on occasion, but she let it go and simply came to the next meeting. She found the group over time treated her with more respect and even asked her opinion on occasion. Finally, at her suggestion they were able to make some new choices about how to use the endowment funds to support ministry more effectively. Of course, shifts in how congregations or small trustee boards or finance committees make financial decisions do not happen overnight. Even beginning to make the shifts takes time.

Make sure you look at the strengths as well as the negatives in your church's functioning around money. What are the positive elements in how they handle their resources? What can you celebrate about the way church leaders have dealt with money matters over the years and decades? Where do those strengths come from in their history? Some churches have a long history of giving away substantial sums of money for mission endeavors. Others have clear and effective ways of cultivating giving in their members. Perhaps your church has always had open and reliable record-keeping, or a tradition of encouraging gifts to an endowment to support ministry. Obviously, some churches do better than others at raising money, managing it, spending it, and giving it away. Yet every church which still has its doors open has strengths to celebrate.

Of course, there may be real challenges in any or all of these areas that need to be addressed right away. Still, the more positive you can be about what you see in your own congregation, the more effective you can be at leading them and helping them both to build on the strengths and to handle the difficulties. When you can genuinely celebrate aspects of their financial life, you will have a different relationship with lay leaders and church members as you work together to support the life of the congregation. If they know you appreciate who they are and their hard work over the years in maintaining their life together, they will be more open to your leadership.

You may find the tips on the following page useful as you work with your congregation on issues related to money. Applying them will take more than a few weeks or months. Consider this a long-term research project which will support and enhance your ministry in this congregation.

✓

Tips for Church Leaders on Relating to the History of Your Church

I
Read any written histories your church has produced. Look for hints about its approach to money over the years.

2
Ask the oldest members of the church for their understanding of how the congregation has dealt with money in their memory. Compare their stories with the written history.

3
Assess what is going on in the present for its connection with the past. Watch for similarities and differences. Is there growth or regression (not just in dollar amounts, but also in the ability to deal with challenge)?

4
Pay attention to particularly significant events, positive or negative: a large bequest, a new building, a building fire, embezzlement, or a church split. The residue of past milestones will be present in the church now in some way. Notice whether people never talk about them, or talk about nothing else (both a sign of intensity).

5
Look for strengths in the history: the founding of the church, success in responding to a budget challenge, building a new ministry or physical plant. Highlight these successes, without trying to be a cheerleader.

6
Observe the role of the pastor in the money life of the church. Does the leadership depend heavily on you, or leave you out? Research your predecessors and how they functioned in this area of church life (both what they say and what others say about them).

SHARING THE STORY

How should you share the fruits of your research? You might tell the stories you learn about the church's money story from time to time to key leaders, to the whole board or vestry, and even to the congregation as a whole. It could make for an interesting one-time sermon. Try not to anxiously criticize or harangue: "This church has *never* supported its pastors well!" Be aware of your own stance, and do not position yourself as the know-it-all telling them something about their own church and its money. Instead, stand with them as a fellow learner who loves their church, too. Gently put the story in front of people, whether it is one of struggle or strength or both: "Here are some things I've been learning about our church finances lately." Or, "Mildred was just telling me something interesting about the church budget I hadn't heard before." If there is difficult history, rather than making people face their past history, see it as a way to open the door to future conversation. You might say, "Hmm, I noticed this—what do you think about it?" You are giving people a chance to reflect on their own story, now or when they are ready in the future. When you are calmly honest about both strengths and weaknesses, you allow room for shifts to happen.

Sharing your learnings with others can be enjoyable, especially when you unearth unexpected resources and strengths. Do it in a positive manner, as a way of tapping into the collective wisdom and resources. You can use the stories of the past to encourage people in the present. James Lamkin of Northside Drive Baptist Church in Atlanta says that in facing the recent economic crisis he found in his research that his church also dealt with recessionary times in the 1970s. He made a copy of the church newsletter from 1975 about budget cutbacks and layoffs. He asked his leaders, "How in the world did the church handle this crisis? It looks worse then than it is now." He reminded them of the resourcefulness the church had shown in the past that was still available in the present. He says, "It's like sliding Grandpa's picture in front of the family and saying, he was a rascal, but he had tenacity, don't you think?"[3] It is possible to frame even past difficulties as a sign of resourcefulness: this church is still standing, still worshipping, still maintaining its building, and that is something to celebrate.

Finally, be patient. It's easy to think if you simply point out the negative practices to folks, or describe a better way of doing things, that everything will change. "Isn't it obvious?" we think. Yet because the patterns come out of the deeper "logic" of emotional process over decades of relationships, rational argument does not often change anything. And in one way, these behaviors have worked: the institution is still alive. Sure, there might be more productive, more economical, less conflictual ways of doing the church's business. Yet people do what they do for a reason. "Mr. Johnson always pays the bill at the end of the year, so why do we need to challenge others to give? It's worked for us." "We have not needed the pastor's input to the trustees; we've managed fine so far without it, so why do we need you?" People do not ask these questions explicitly, of course, and they may not even be aware of them. The questions are at work nonetheless, and a wise leader is aware of them. Remember, church patterns that have developed over many decades, and even centuries in some cases, will not go away simply because some pastor or priest says they should. Expect to take some years to create the kind of shifts in functioning around money that will last. To see changes that will last beyond your own tenure may take the rest of your ministry. Imagine how your church's financial life might be in thirty years, or one hundred. Then take some small actions now that can have a big impact over time.

Every congregation is fascinating, and every church's history is fascinating when you begin to approach it as a resource for your own leadership in the area of money and for the congregation's financial present and future. Appropriate humility and respect are necessary qualities. Sometimes clergy come in and act as if the past is worthless and only the future (done their way) matters. The church may face real financial issues that need to be addressed. All congregations need to adapt to survive financially and institutionally in a changing environment. You may need to have difficult conversations and make difficult choices. Leaders who begin from a position of respect for others, and who put in the time (on the clock and on the calendar) to sit with folks and listen to the stories will have more capital to draw on when leaders face challenging choices. People will not feel backed into a corner.

Can you bring an open heart to your church's story, and where it is now on its journey with money? Can you deeply accept where they are and where they have been? Perhaps their values are different from your values. Sure, you would like to see them grow in giving and in freedom from the materialism of our society, and not just so they can pay you a better salary. You are a spiritual leader and you want more for them and for the ministry than you all have right now. Still, a leader who stands tapping his or her foot waiting for people to get it and come along will not go far in motivating those who follow. People respond to leaders who both love and accept them as they are, while over time challenging them to see a bigger picture of what is possible.

IDEAS TO PONDER

Remember, it takes a long time to get to know a congregation and its history. Do not expect to get there in a year. After a year you may have an idea of where to begin, and it takes at least five years to understand the lay of the land in a congregation. With a high-valence topic such as money, it may take longer to get the picture, especially if you yourself are anxious about it, too. Celebrate the strengths of the past; acknowledge and accept the challenges that have been handed down. Roll up your sleeves and get to work, together with others, to craft a thoughtful approach to the present and the future. It could be fun.

◆ Questions

Here are seven questions to ask about your church's money story.

1. How did the church get started? How was it funded at the beginning? What can you learn about how the founders dealt with money, including the founding pastor?

2. What has been the pattern of support over the years? Annual giving? Endowment (and how was it created)? Denominational subsidy?

3. What financial crises has the church faced? How has the congregation weathered them?

4. Are there particular areas of ministry, now and in the past, that become the focus of people's anxiety about money: the building? staffing? mission/outreach giving?

5. Who knows what about the money? Has that always been the case? How much secrecy or openness do you see?

6. Where are the financial records archives kept, and who knows what is in them?

7. What are the long-term patterns related to stewardship: is giving going up or down? If there has been a shift in either direction, when did it take place? What else was going on in the congregation at the time?

chapter five

Remember Your Family's Money Story

*To the extent that the pastor has not resolved issues
about money related to his or her family of origin,
the pastor will never be able to resolve issues
about money in his or her congregation.*

— Israel Galindo, Columbia Theological Seminary[1]

SOMETIMES THE MONEY patterns in your church that
you perceive as problematic will be so frustrating you will want
to tear your hair out. Other times they may seem charming. This
may have more to do with your own level of anxiety, in general
and around money in particular, than with anything objective
about the church. We all need to recognize our own contribution
to challenges around money at church. The way we react to financial matters at church is rooted in our experience in the families we grew up in. Frank, the pastor of a small Disciples church,
led the congregation to sell their building to another church,
with the proviso that they could continue to use the building for
worship as long as they wanted. Church members had a hard
time accepting that they no longer owned the building. Frank
found the transition was not difficult for him. Thinking back,
he remembered his parents had never owned a home, and were
always comfortable in rental housing. Suddenly, it made sense
that he would be happy leading a church which worshipped in
someone else's building.

KNOW YOUR FAMILY'S
RELATIONSHIP TO MONEY

Your own family's money story has a deep impact on how you lead in church finance, because you learn the meaning of money in the family you grow up in. One pastor remembers hearing his mother say, every time they saw someone driving a nice car, "But are they happy?" We internalize any number of lines, from "Money doesn't grow on trees" to "You can't take it with you." It is in your family of origin that you learned what you now believe and practice about work, about spending, about saving, about borrowing. Some of the lessons are spoken out loud; other messages are given silently yet no less powerfully.

Of course, families also teach lessons about giving. Bill Enright is now director of the Lake Institute on Faith and Giving, and for many years was a Presbyterian pastor. He says, "I grew up in a family where we were taught to give." He tells the story of saving for a $30 red Schwinn bike out of his first paper route. When he had the $30, he told his mother he was going to buy the bike. She asked him, "Did you pay your tithe?" He says, "I had to work another couple of weeks to get the bike."[2] You remember for a lifetime what you learn from your parents about giving.

When you grow up, those family patterns are still present. You may follow the same way of dealing with money, or you may react and do the opposite. Perhaps you spend lavishly like your father, or take a vow never to put the family finances at risk the way he did. Your birth order and other circumstances in your growing up life affect how you live out the family's money story. But whether you slavishly follow the family script or rebel against it, that story has a powerful impact on your relationship with money. If you marry and have children, you create a nuclear family of your own, and in turn teach your children lessons about money.

Many clergy are not comfortable talking about money, and this is often rooted in their family experience. Many of us did not learn how to manage or even discuss money in the families we grew up in. Bill Enright works with groups of clergy around the country doing seminars on churches and giving. He always asks, "How many of you grew up in families where you talked about money?" Typically, Enright says, in a group of twenty-five participants, about four hands will go up. He gets a similar response to the question, "How many of you knew how much your parents gave?"[3] When you do not learn a vocabulary of money—or of stewardship—early in your life, you can find it difficult to lead a congregation to have more open conversations about money or to boldly challenge people to give more.

An important way to gain greater freedom in your relationship with money, both at home and at church, is to explore your family's relationship with it through the generations. You can become a student of the multigenerational process that has shaped you and the way you deal with finances. Over time, this can help you become clearer and more intentional about your own choices in relation to money and to other people around money matters. As you step back from the automatic forces at work in you, you can find yourself more thoughtful and less reactive about money.

How to begin this work? Here's one way to start to explore the patterns you can see and the stories and conversations you remember hearing about money in your family of origin. Begin by simply looking at your family and trying to assess what the patterns are. You can track money matters in your own family by developing a family diagram or genogram.[4] Then take a look to see, over at least three generations, what people have done for work and how they have done financially. Begin to wonder what has been the general family attitude toward money. How important is financial success? What do the family leaders, the patriarchs and the matriarchs, think about money and what do they do with it?

As you examine your family story, remember that money in family life, like church life, is not a thing in itself. It becomes a focus for the family, a way to absorb the free-floating anxiety that comes with the territory of being human. This can show up in any number of ways in families. A spouse who is unable to earn a living. Constant conflict between spouses about how to spend the money they have. Or complete avoidance of conversations about finances. Some families have a designated financial success, often the oldest. And there may be a family member who struggles to make enough to live on, often someone further down the birth order, a younger daughter or a younger son. What do you notice in your family about where anxiety shows up in relation to money? This work is best done with a coach in an individual or small group setting where you look at your family genogram and begin to position yourself in a different place in your family over time. It's easier to have some help to know where to begin and what to do if you get stuck. This is not a quick-fix model for change, but a long-term process of exploration.

If your parents are still living, you can ask them questions about how they learned about money. You don't need to give them the third degree, but just ask a question now and again. This can be part of your ongoing reflective research on your own family. Listen with different ears to the stories people tell. My father has started talking in recent years (or perhaps I'm just listening better now) about the fact that his father did not think he should go to college on the GI Bill after World War II, but should take up a trade. Dad ended up not only going to college but sending some of the stipend he received home to help support his parents. He sent money home until he married in his thirties. This kind of family exploration can make the obligatory visits home much more interesting and a richer experience for everyone. Of course, in some families with big money traumas like bankruptcy, a business failure, or inheritance struggles that lead to emotional cutoff, raising questions about the past is not easy. It can take a long time to be ready to even begin these conversations.

Take a look at your family genogram and see what information you don't know. You can ask questions like, "What kind of work did Grandpa do?" or, "How did you decide to be an engineer?" or, "Did your parents give you an allowance?" Your parents do not have to be living to begin this exploration. If you still have aunts or uncles, you can use them as a resource. In addition, cousins can be a great source of information about the family's money story, and as peers can be easier to approach than the previous generation. The information you get from any family member may be new and valuable. But more important, you are standing in your family in a different way, as a researcher, just as you can do with your congregation. When you are doing this research, you can be more neutral, less inclined to be caught up in the emotional patterns of your family or to be judgmental, annoyed, or slavishly loyal to one member or another.

LEARNING TO MAKE DIFFERENT CHOICES

Why take the time to do this work? Not only can it give you more freedom in your personal financial life, it can also help you with the money side of ministry. Your family's money story affects your leadership, and when you have more perspective on how you were shaped in relation to money, you will have greater freedom in the money side of ministry. When you work on some of the difficult issues related to money in your family of origin, you will find it far easier to deal with money in ministry and in life. Your family is always available to you (no matter who is no longer living or geographically distant) as you do this work of understanding in greater depth the forces that have shaped you in relationship to money. As you learn, you can begin to bring your new perspective into your awareness of your own financial functioning. Awareness is not everything, but it is a start. See if you can notice more about how you make your own money decisions, compared with the rest of your family and previous generations. When you make these observations, different choices become possible over time.

Mark, a Presbyterian minister, realized as he looked at his own family that he was the golden boy in his family. His father was the oldest in his family, but had struggled to provide for the family. As a result, there was even more pressure on him, as the oldest in the next generation, to do well. He was the firstborn of the cousins in that generation, too. He chose ministry, not a highly-paid profession, but he ended up in a big, prestigious church which paid well. He felt a lot of pressure to keep the church finances on track. He was what is sometimes known as a "standard-bearer" for the family, often if not always male, who has to succeed for more than one generation of a family. For Mark, it showed up most intensely in finances. Over time, he was able to lower his own expectations of himself a little— and that little went a long way toward reducing his stress.

As you learn more about the family forces that have created your attitudes toward money, you can develop more neutrality toward it, and have more options. This is not an easy process, and it is not a quick one. It's a gradual shift. The old patterns are always ready to resurface in times of high anxiety, when we often revert to the ways of functioning we learned in childhood. Still, if you are aware of what you do when you are anxious, you will have more choices. Your responses will be less automatic. When the treasurer calls you in a panic, after an initially anxious response, you may be better able to step back and have a thoughtful conversation.

Sue, a Methodist minister in a small congregation, was not the oldest, but she was the oldest girl. She did not feel the pressure to produce, but she felt internal pressure to take care of others. Her younger sister struggled financially, and Sue sometimes sent her money to tide her over. When transients stopped by the church and asked for money, she had a hard time saying no, even though the church had a clear policy about not giving out cash. She felt guilty every time, and sometimes she just gave out her own money. She began to look at her family story, and realized that her mother also had a sister who struggled with finances. She had forgotten about the whispered conversations her parents had had about whether they could afford to send money to Aunt Judy. In conversation with her mother she discovered that Judy was in a nursing home a few hours from her church. Her parents were still in touch with her, although she herself had not seen Judy since she was a kid. She made a visit at a time when her mother was going to be there. Soon after that she told her sister she would not be able to send money anymore. Her sister was angry for a short time and quit speaking to her, but settled down by Christmas when the family got together. And she found herself much more able to be calm about people asking her for money, and able to implement the church policy of never giving cash.

Family systems theory suggests that it is better to view the family as a whole rather than focusing on the problems of an individual. What happens between people is as important as what happens inside people. You learn how to relate to others and to the world at large—and to money—out of the family you grew up in. Your parents had parents, and they learned how to relate to others out of those family experiences, and this pattern goes on back through the generations. So the more you learn about your parents and previous generations and how they related to money, the more you learn about yourself and the more you gain options for engaging with money, and with other people around money. You may say, "How can this be? These events happened so long ago. I've never even heard of any of those people. How can their lives affect me and how I relate to money?" It may simply be that your grandmother passed down some of her anxieties to your father, and your father passed them down to you in turn as he raised you. However it happens, I never cease to be amazed by the way patterns from the past show up in the present in complex and subtle ways.

In my own family there are multiple generations of high anxiety about money. My father was caught in an intense triangle with his parents. His father did not like to work for other people, and he had a small roofing business. He worked just enough to pay the bills. My grandmother was always anxious about money, since she was deprived of an inheritance as a young woman. She recruited my father to try to get his father to work harder and earn more. My grandfather would say to my father, "I've got two pensions; I don't know what she wants." He was content as long as the bills were paid, but she could never feel secure because of her own intense story. And my father was caught in the middle. My father, learning his lesson well from his mother, hates to spend money. He has accumulated substantial assets as a result of his frugality and his long career working. My cousins have told me that his older brother, my uncle, would spend any money he had. They had different responses to the family anxiety about money. Like my father, I'm inclined to be frugal and to worry about whether there will be enough.

Exploring my family story has made a difference for me. One year I invited my father and my brother to meet me in Kansas, and we visited the towns where my father was born and grew up. We visited the farm that my grandmother and her siblings inherited and then lost due to her brother-in-law's mismanagement, according to my father's long-ago memories. We went to the cemetery where her parents were buried following their tragic death. I believe many of the roots of our family anxiety about money lie in that town. Following the visit some things shifted for me and for the family. My father suddenly offered to buy me a car, the most spontaneously generous thing he has ever done for me. My husband and I bought our first home after living in a parsonage for years. And we were also able to make some decisions about investing an inheritance he received that year.

The shifts seemed almost magical. And yet I can't say it is magic. Years later, I still am slow to make decisions about money. I try to practice what I preach, and I notice I can only do it sometimes. I know from the inside out how hard it is to take action on some of these matters. As I have explored the history of money in my family, and observed others across the generations and the way they relate to it, I have found I do have more choices. In my pastoral ministry, I found myself over time much more able to be straightforward about money matters and to lead in stewardship without apology. In family life I am more able to have conversations about money rather than avoiding them. It's not a magic bullet—I still have to work hard to regulate my anxiety about money. And like my father, I'm still checking to see if this shaving cream is a quarter cheaper than the other.

I have worked over the years, and continue to work to cultivate in myself the ability to be more thoughtful about money, make decisions about it that are based in my values, think clearly about money rather than getting fuzzy from anxiety, ask for and receive what my work is worth, trust God more fully, be lighter and less serious about money, and celebrate every day the wealth

I do have. I have found it valuable to connect with more distant branches of the family to relate with people who have different values and make different choices in relation to money, as a way to extend my repertoire in this challenging area of life. What would you like to develop in yourself in relation to money? And where in your family might you find people who have those attitudes?

Finally, don't forget that families bring strengths as well as difficulties in the area of money. If your family fed you, kept a roof over your head, and provided clothes for your back, they had some ability to manage resources. You might make a list of the financial resources your family had and have. Don't stop with your parents—think about your grandparents and great-grandparents. Israel Galindo remembers that his own immigrant family had a multigenerational tradition of a strong work ethic. He says, "They never had huge anxieties about money because their work ethic is, you take responsibility for doing what you need to do to take care of your family. They always had a strong sense of agency, that issues about money are under our control." He sees that as a significant resource in his own life.[5] Look at your family and see what you can celebrate about how they related to money: They paid the bills. They knew how to spend money to have a good time. They saved regularly. They were generous with others.

One of the Ten Commandments says, "Honor your father and your mother." I gained a great deal from my parents and from their families that helps me in relation to money every day. I know how to live frugally, which can give a lot of freedom. I understand the value of giving. I place a high value on being independent and standing on my own two feet. Of course, I inherited some challenges, too: high anxiety and difficulty in making financial decisions. But I am grateful for the gifts which have helped me all my life. What can you name in your own family story that is worth celebrating?

Tips for Exploring Your Family's Money Story

1

Write one page that expresses what you learned from your family of origin about money. Read it over to see how that learning gets expressed in your ministry (for better and for worse).

2

Ask your parents individually, if they are living, what they learned from their parents about money. Stay curious rather than judgmental in this conversation. Have it in person if possible.

3

Observe how your siblings and cousins deal with money. Is it different from or the same as the way you deal with it?

4

Assess your connection with your extended family. Are you connected with the most financially successful person (and do you know who that is)? What about the least financially successful? Notice the family attitudes toward these people.

5

Notice the attitude toward gift-giving in your family. Is it balanced, or do some give more than others? Are gifts freely given, or is there a sense of obligation? What has been the attitude toward charitable giving?

6

Consider the strengths you received from your family in this area. They may come quickly to mind, or you may have to think hard. Even if your values and approach to money differ sharply from your family, see if you can generate at least one idea.

One caveat: don't engage with your family in the area of money with the intention of fixing them. If you step back into your family in relation to money with your usual overfunctioning role, you will not bring yourself or anyone else to greater freedom. It is not selfish to engage with your family for your own growth and freedom. The paradox is that the more you can be free of your need to fix them financially, the more freedom they can have to find their own way to greater freedom and possibility. You are not their pastor, their social worker, or their therapist. You are son, daughter, brother, sister. You don't do your family a lot of good when you anxiously try to help them. I spent plenty of energy trying to convince my parents, especially my father, to spend more money on their own comfort, and I don't think I ever convinced my dad to spend one more dollar. In fact, I realized that one of the ways my father shows love is by giving us items he has obtained for free. That epiphany shifted my attitude from annoyance to openness. Now I can gratefully receive these items—a candle, a jar of pickles, a tote bag—as expressions of his love. It is a privilege to accept them. Rather than trying to change him (at the age of ninety!), I am far more able to accept who he is and how he relates to spending and not spending money.

It is easy to be judgmental about family members and their relationship with money: "They're irresponsible!" "They're materialistic!" "They're cheap!" To engage in the ongoing work of differentiation means letting go of judgment, at least for a time. You are observing, and focusing on yourself and your place in the family. This does not mean you give up your values. Rather, you begin to acknowledge that there may be more going on in the family over the generations than you realized. Brother Bob, who can't seem to hold a job, is filling a position in the family—somehow every generation seems to have somebody shiftless. Sister Sue, who has been on welfare, is following the pattern that every youngest daughter seems to follow. Older brother Tom, who is a corporate king-maker, is just doing what oldest brothers do. More is at work than birth order, of course, but it is one element in how families function. And you—you are the "good" one, the one who went into ministry. You, too, are filling a role.

This is not a bad thing: it is just what families do. And when you can see the patterns, it can be easier to let go of the scripts that go round and round in your head and sometimes come out of your mouth. "I can't believe you're still living with Mom!" You might even be able to say, "I'm so glad you're able to be at home and help Mom out." Letting go of judgments about family members and their relationship with their money can be a way to mature spiritually as well as emotionally.

You may find that your family may be a resource for you in ways you had not thought about it. Perhaps you have a brother who left the church altogether. He has focused his attention on his business, and you have always viewed him as the black sheep, and a bit materialistic. But when the church has a financial challenge, he might serve as a sounding board for you. It could shift your relationship with him. Instead of assuming he needs you more than you need him, you relate to him as someone who could help you. And he might have a useful perspective for you, especially if you find the business side of church a challenge.

Who are the people in your family who know the most about money, and how might you connect with them? You may find that you have been occupying a position (the spiritual one who knows nothing about money, for example). Perhaps as things shift, you find you are more interested in money than you thought. Or your brother can become an ongoing resource for you, a valued adviser in ways you never thought possible. You might find a new relationship with a cousin you haven't seen since childhood who is an accountant and the treasurer of her church.

What will help you in your ministry leadership around money is greater maturity, or differentiation of self, as Murray Bowen termed it. Greater emotional and spiritual maturity is essential for leadership, especially in a hot area like money. Maturity means you know who you are and are able to act out of that identity in relationship with others, without losing yourself. You know where you end and other people begin. You know your own principles and values in relation to money, and you can allow others to have their own perspective without trying to change them. It's not easy work but it is fruitful, over time. Count the time in years, not months, although occasionally there can be a big breakthrough.

When money issues come up in the congregation, go back to your family genogram and see if you can see parallels. If you are feeling anxious about money, Ed Bacon, rector of All Saints Episcopal Church in Pasadena, suggests you constantly ask, "What's going on in my family of origin now, or what has been triggered about how I was set up in my family of origin?" This is a regular practice he himself has in his ministry.[6] It can be useful to have someone to walk through this process with you, a thoughtful friend or a coach who is trained in family systems thinking. There can be a double payoff for doing this kind of family work: greater emotional freedom in your own financial life, and greater freedom in your leadership in relation to money at church.

Bacon suggests you can even invite church members to have conversations about their own family stories: "It's liberating to find your partners in the church who are willing to talk with you about that. It is amazing how storytelling calms anxiety, or reduces anxiety. To get people to start talking about that all of a sudden shifts the focus to self rather than blaming others, and self-criticism rather than criticizing something external."[7] You might ask members of the finance committee or trustees to spend a meeting telling these stories, or have one person share something at the beginning of each meeting. As you tell some of your own story and listen to the stories of others, you set the stage for more reflective leadership around finances.

A little more freedom goes a long way in ministry and in family life. Martha, a Lutheran pastor, spent several years exploring this intense area of family life, asking her parents questions about their relationship with money and what they remembered about their own parents and grandparents. Over time, she found herself much more able to be up-front about money in church and at home. She asked for a raise instead of passively taking what she was offered. She was more straightforward about stewardship from the pulpit. She was able to have different conversations with her young adult children about their requests for money. The more mature you are, the more options you have and the less compulsive your behavior is. Whether your automatic tendency is to be a saver or a spender, as you grow you can be more aware of what you are doing and adapt to fit the circumstances—saving, spending, and giving as appropriate.

Leaders who are more mature are less likely to be caught up in the anxiety of others about a potential giving shortfall. They are more able to act on principle in conversation about the budget without being rigid. They are better able to relate to leaders and members about money matters in a way that calls forth the best thinking in others. They are less likely to be manipulated or coerced by the least mature, and that is in the best interests of everyone. They are less likely to be tripped up by their own family patterns around money. And the bottom-line results in the funding of ministry can be real. Pastors who are freer to talk about money are less afraid to ask for it and to minister to people in the area of their financial lives.

GROW IN YOUR OWN RELATIONSHIP TO MONEY

As you reflect on your money story and cultivate a greater openness in the way you relate to money, you can find a shift in the way you handle your own financial life. Your focus on money can become noticeably less anxious. Furthermore, bringing a thoughtful consciousness to personal financial management will help your leadership, because you will truly be putting your money where your mouth is. You will be clearer and calmer when preaching, teaching, and providing administrative leadership about finances.

On the other hand, when you have a hard time managing your own money, you will experience increased anxiety about budget matters at church. This makes you a less effective financial leader in your congregation. If you have large consumer or educational debt and are struggling to make your payments, it will be hard to be free when you are preaching about money. If you are resentful because your salary does not cover your expenses, it will be hard to be free when you are sitting in a budget meeting. If you cannot pay attention to your own budget, it will be hard to bring attentive awareness to the church reports. Furthermore, it can limit others' growth in this area. It is a principle that you cannot lead others beyond your own level of maturity. Does this mean that you have to put your financial life in order completely before you can lead people to work on their own financial issues? No. But you have to work on your own growth in this area if you are asking others to do so; otherwise, your words will have less impact.

Tips for Dealing with Your Personal Finances

1
Learn about personal finance. Find a mentor in this critical area.

2
Observe your own spending patterns, without trying to change them. What can you learn about yourself?

3
Calculate your net worth. Do this every year, recognizing that the total, whether large or small, does not reflect your human worth.

4
View your money as a resource for life, now and in the future. Don't ignore it, and don't spend all your time thinking or worrying about it.

5
Talk with your family about your own values and goals around money. Have a conversation with your spouse and children, if any, about their thinking in this area.

Working on a mature relationship to money is challenging at all times, and more challenging when there is a partner involved. As you look at your finances, it can be useful to reflect on the triangles that are at work in your immediate family relationships. You are in multiple triangles around your personal finances, as well. Here are a few family triangles related to money:

◆ with your spouse and the church

◆ with your spouse and any children you have

◆ with your spouse and money itself (this triangle can become an intense marital triangle)

◆ with your spouse and your parents (or in-laws).

If you are single, it may be simpler but not necessarily easier. You must support yourself on your own, and that can be a source of anxiety. You might look at your family story and see where the single people are and what kind of choices they made. How did they take care of themselves, or did someone else do so? What happened at the end of their lives? And reflect on the triangles with extended family and with your children if you have them.

Remember the principles of triangles again: for example, you cannot control anyone else's relationship with money. Rather, you can define yourself around what you believe about money ("I'd like to see us save more this year") instead of trying to will or control them ("Why can't you just relax and spend the money on this vacation?"). In some partnerships money is too far on the outside, and partners do not spend enough time dealing with it (this has been a difficulty at times in my own marriage). And, of course, both partners come from families of origin that affect their functioning around money, often in very different ways. It is easy to be judgmental about a partner's money habits when he or she may simply have a different style of relating to money. If you have an intense and conflicted relationship with money, and your partner has a distant relationship with money, you have one kind of triangle to deal with in the relationship. If you are passive and distant from money matters, and your partner spends freely, you have another one.

It is important to get enough distance to know what it is you do in relation to money within your marriage. What sets you off in the relationship regarding money? What makes you most anxious? Can you see it happening when it happens, or not until afterwards? Can you be a researcher of your partner and what he or she does, and not react to it? As with church finances, stepping back to get a wider perspective will help you become more thoughtful and begin to make some different choices, if you want to.

Personal financial matters are not just financial, in the way many personal finance books address them. Our challenges are not technical alone; they are emotional and spiritual. The fact is, all the good advice in the world about personal finance will not do any good if you cannot take action—or if you take lots of action while you are thinking anxiously. If you overspend by credit card, postpone necessary investment decisions, or refuse to ask for a raise because people might get upset, you are making anxious choices about money. Forces beyond the rational are driving you. For a shift to happen, you have to look deeper. We have seen some ways to do this in gaining perspective on your family story, and later in the book we will consider spiritual elements of this journey. When you grow, emotionally and spiritually, you find greater freedom. This includes financial freedom. More maturity means you have more choices rather than being governed by anxiety and fear, or by old family patterns. You can take thoughtful action rather than reacting or taking no action at all.

Consider having the goal of being less anxious about money. I know I am never going to be non-anxious, especially about money, but I *am* less anxious about it than I used to be. I am more able to plan and to make decisions about it. Money "has me" less than it used to, and I am freer. Lowering your anxiety about money even a little goes a long way, both at church and in personal life. You can see more options and be more creative as you manage your money and yourself. When you are calmer, you will find it easier to take a steady and thoughtful approach to managing your own money.

Here are three ways to work on managing money anxiety. First, *monitor your spending and your time spent on money matters.* As you pay attention, you may find yourself shifting your habits. Growth in this area will look different for different people. For some, lowered anxiety will mean spending less, as they find less need to shop to prop themselves up. For others, lowered anxiety may mean spending more, and not hoarding their money. For some, it will mean taking more time every week on finances, as they pay more attention rather than zoning out. For others, it means taking *less* time, as they don't feel the need to hover over their investments.

Second, *monitor your intake of media reports on the national and international financial picture.* They will not help you think more clearly about your own finances. If you are a news junkie, experiment with taking in a little less. Turn off the radio or set your home page to a non-news site. The media designs its news offerings to get your attention by raising your anxiety, and spending a lot of time with them will not help you.

Third, *cultivate a different perspective on your resources.* Most of us have more than we think we have, not only finan- cially but in other ways. I am trying to develop a global perspec- tive on my own resources. James E. Hughes is an attorney who works with families with significant wealth. While most clergy are not wealthy, Hughes's recommendations for how families think through their own values could be applied by any family or individual. He suggests that families have three types of cap- ital: human, intellectual, and financial. *Human capital* is the people in your family. (He means extended family, not just nu- clear family.) *Intellectual capital* is the collective knowledge of the family, through life experience and other learning. Of course, *financial capital* is the family's tangible resources. So if you think about your family from this perspective, you may see that you have more wealth than you thought.[8] Hughes's model is another way to get above the fray of your anxiety about money to see what assets your family have, and what is most important to you. Take some time to reflect on your extended family and the resources you bring to each other and the world.

IDEAS TO PONDER

A spirit of celebration of the resources you do have can help you move toward greater freedom in your financial life. When you begin with a sense of having enough, you reframe conversations and decision-making about money. Just as in congregational life, celebrating what you have creates far more energy than worrying or bemoaning what you do not have. This can be a daily, enjoyable practice: simply notice and appreciate what you do have. Celebrate the "capital" you see in your own extended family, in the families you know, and in your church's life, past and present. You will not lack for material, if you begin to open your eyes. Cultivate a global perspective on your resources: whatever your circumstances, you likely have far more than most people around the globe.

◆　*Questions*

Here are eight questions to consider as you do your own research on your family relationship with money.

1. What does money mean in your family?

2. Who is the most responsible person in your family around money? the least?

3. Do you earn more or less than your siblings? What about your cousins?

4. What do you notice about gender and money, if anything?

5. How do people in your extended family make decisions about money? What values and criteria do they use? Does your immediate family differ from the extended family?

6. What is the general attitude toward philanthropy and stewardship?

7. How did you learn about money growing up? How did your parents learn? What did your spouse learn?

8. What is the meaning of success in your family?

chapter six

Learn to Handle Money Challenges

Money is the oxygen that is necessary to the metabolism of the whole body to function. It is necessary in order for any body of believers to express its purpose in their context. Oxygen is a relatively unstable thing and is potentially very corrosive. It can eat metal and create all kinds of havoc. It's also very explosive. So lots of oxygen in any one place means lots of explosive potential. That's a helpful reminder to me.

— Bob Hunter, former Director of Stewardship,
Second Presbyterian Church, Indianapolis[1]

THE EXPLOSIVE POWER of money is one of the challenges churches face. How we respond is as important as the challenge itself. We have examined a number of key financial difficulties leaders face, and we will look at some more examples in this chapter. Whatever your situation, remember that a thoughtful response makes a better outcome possible. And we have much more control over ourselves than we do over our external circumstances. It's not easy to manage ourselves, yet it is possible.

The African-American folktale "Flossie and the Fox" tells the story of a little girl who encounters a fox on her way through the woods to deliver some eggs. Instead of running away in terror, she acts like she doesn't know what a fox is. As he follows her, Flossie suggests to the fox since he is furry like a rabbit, he must be a rabbit. Then she says his long pointed nose means he must be a rat. He has sharp claws and yellow eyes like a cat they encounter, and a bushy tail like a squirrel in the trees overhead. By the time he suggests to her that he has sharp teeth and can run very fast, she is out of the woods, and points out to the fox that the dogs about to come after him also have sharp teeth and can run fast. And Flossie reaches her destination safely.[2]

Flossie's story suggests one approach leaders can take to the volatile nature of financial problems: Don't take it so seriously. She faces a situation of real danger—a little girl alone with a fox. But she courageously uses her imagination to poke fun at the fox, and distracts him from his purpose long enough to reach safety. She uses her creativity to disarm the dangerous force. When you respond to a financial challenge too seriously, you tend to disengage your imagination. Options seem narrow (A fox! Run away!) or nonexistent (We'll all be killed!). Fight-or-flight reflexes kick in. At the same time, a broader repertoire of responses can increase the possibility of survival. Reframing, playing dumb for a time, looking for an alternative path through the thick woods, calling on the resources of others: all may be useful strategies if you can remain calm enough to see them. Responding to danger with a variety of actions, including humor, is not the same as denial. Those who are most anxious may view it that way: "Can't you see the sky is falling?" they may cry. "You're just not taking it seriously enough!" Yet part of the task of leadership is to offer your followers a bigger picture and a longer perspective.

The more you can keep your head, the better you can imagine options. The foxes of this world, external and internal, will be less likely to steal your resourcefulness and keep you from reaching your goals. We have all faced the effects of financial foxes in recent years, and there are real consequences to their actions. But your survival, as with Flossie, depends as much or more on your own responses and resourcefulness as it does on external forces. How can you cultivate the kind of response that can make a difference in challenging financial circumstances? Whether your church is facing a budget crisis, an ongoing decline in funding for ministry, or the need to develop resources for a new ministry initiative, you can work on your own internal clarity, your reactions, and your connections with others. Here are some qualities of those who are mature about money, who have the resources that can help them navigate almost any financial challenge or crisis:

- Have an ability to focus on and celebrate the positive without denying challenges;
- Are not too attached to outcome;
- Are not too attached to what people think of them;
- Are able to take a stand for themselves around salary and other financial matters;
- Can challenge others to give, without apology;
- Can tolerate others being angry with them;
- Are not too anxious about the ups and downs in their financial life or the church's life;
- Can take responsibility for personal finances, and can make decisions and manage themselves around money;
- Have an appropriately lighthearted approach to money, taking money seriously enough, but not too seriously.

Some people have a natural ability in these areas. Most of us do not. Whatever your tendency, however, you can develop yourself in the direction of more flexibility, more clarity, and lowered anxiety. It takes time, and it requires real persistence. Still, the payoff (emotional as much as financial) is real and valuable, for yourself and for your congregation—not to mention your family. Leadership around finances is not easy, yet it can become *easier* for yourself and other key leaders around you. You do not have to let either the ongoing anxiety or the panic of a crisis govern your behavior. You do not have to allow your responses to be determined by the actions of others. There are always options.

Now, let's get more specific. Every church over time will face a multitude of large and small challenges related to money. Here are some questions and answers about issues that may come up in church. You may have asked one or more of these questions, or your issues may be different. But when you learn to bring a systems perspective to money issues, then you will be better able to apply this thinking to your own setting as matters arise over time. It is not about a specific technique; rather, it is a way of thinking about how people relate to each other around money, and how you bring yourself to your leadership in this critical area of church life.

◆ *What if our biggest giver dies?*
Ideally, consider this question before it happens. One way to address this before the fact is to make sure you have information on the pledge numbers—not just totals, but dollars per individual pledge. Even if you don't (yet) know the names, you should know the numbers. If there's one pledge which seems to be the largest by far, you can take this up with the leadership. "If this pledge goes away for any reason, we're going to be in trouble." A midwestern church in a small community had one couple who gave $2,000 per week. When he died, she reduced her pledge to $1,000 a week, forcing the church to find another $52,000 for the budget. After her death, they faced another $50,000 hole, which they "solved" by taking money from the endowment to maintain their ministry. Having an angel in the congregation who underwrites large parts of the budget may seem to be a blessing, but this is a kind of overfunctioning that can lead to a real crisis in the case of an unexpected death or other change in circumstance.

After a key death like this, it's time to have some candid conversation about how the church supports its ministry: "I'm grateful for all Bob did for this church. At the same time, we've allowed Bob to carry us, and he's not here to do that anymore." Do this first with the finance committee and the board, and, if appropriate in your polity, with the congregation. Keep your anxiety down; simply listen, and allow leaders to take responsibility for their own future. Say what you think and what you want as part of the conversation—but listen as much as you talk. This loss of income is a challenge, but it is not your problem to solve alone.

◆ *What if we have a mortgage for our new church, and the funds are not coming in from the capital campaign?*
In all situations where money is tight, anxiety goes up. When there's a church mortgage involved, this may be even more of a tendency. Buildings can be a focus for anxiety. One congregation faced this problem after a big church fight which led to many members leaving. So in addition to the financial challenges, there was the fall-out from a church split. In this case, a new pastor had to come in and deal with both.

As always, responding in a thoughtful way means you and others are more likely to generate solutions. When you can lower your anxiety (and your fight-or-flight automatic reaction) you and others will be more likely to access the more resourceful and creative parts of your brains. Focus more on yourself than on others. While it's not easy to regulate yourself, it takes far less energy than worrying about what others are doing or might do in the future. Bob Hunter points out that when anxiety increases, most people tend to automatically focus on others: "I wish those people would do more to alleviate this difficult time we're experiencing."[3] In this case, it's easy to say, "If only people would complete their pledge to the campaign, we wouldn't have this crisis." And others may be blaming you: "If the pastor were a better leader/more empathetic/a better preacher, people would not be holding back." For the pastoral leader, it becomes a dual discipline—don't blame others, and don't internalize the blame others may be sending your way.

In the midst of all the free-floating anxiety of the crisis, try to remember that you do not need to be the only one to offer the solutions. You may have ideas, but you do not have to solve this problem for the church. It's all right to say, "I'm not sure exactly what to do, but I'm confident we can together come up with some possible solutions." You may have a preferred outcome, but the church's decision is up to them. What is your own bottom line? Be as clear as you can about that, recognizing what you can and cannot control. You can only control yourself and your own anxiety (to a degree). You can frame this as a challenge for the congregation to respond to, and assure them you will walk with them. If you position yourself as a calm, connected leader, they will function better as they address this matter. If you panic or blame or precipitously resign, they will be far less likely to make good decisions about their future. At the same time, their own choices are up to them, and you cannot control them. Be present with them, say what you think, and allow them to make their own decisions.

◆ *What if we don't have enough competent leaders to manage our money?*
Look for the people who are the calmest and most mature. It's better to have a calm person who's not a numbers person as treasurer than an anxious accountant, especially in a smaller church. Maturity generally trumps skill. This doesn't mean skill is irrelevant, but when the heat goes up, you want someone who can keep their head. Furthermore, don't take over too much yourself if it's not your job, whether you are the pastor or a key lay leader. You can support an individual who needs help, but don't do their job for them. This is classic overfunctioning. Of course, you want accurate and competent reports, but the process of encouraging people to take responsibility for their own work is more important than the content of any one report. For the future, leverage your input into the nominating process, and keep your eyes open for possible future leaders who are both skilled and mature. Keep an ongoing list of people you would love to see in financial leadership.

◆ *What if the church is talking about cutting my salary?*
Some churches are faced with the decision of whether they can still afford a full-time pastor or priest. The reality is, the cost of clergy compensation means an increasing number of small churches struggle to pay a full salary. Additionally, many churches with multiple staff have reduced some positions to less than full-time. There are several challenges as church leaders walk through these conversations. First, a pastoral leader needs to look after his or her own interests *and* the best interests of the congregation, which do not always look the same. In a small congregation, the best interests of the church, at least for the short term, may appear to be to reduce to less than full-time

clergy. And the pastor needs a full-time salary. To lead the church through that kind of decision-making process when you are anxious about your own financial survival is not easy. For staff, it can be difficult to negotiate these conversations emotionally. The senior minister may or may not be an advocate for you. Staff can feel in competition for a large enough piece of the salary pie. Whatever your role, it's critical to stay well connected. Stay in touch even with those who may be the loudest voices for a cut. Don't get defensive. Simply state your own position as clearly and calmly as you can in appropriate settings. If you are in a staff position, stay well connected with the minister and any other supervisor you have, as well as key lay people. Watch the triangles.

A second challenge is to function well in your leadership, without overfunctioning. For pastors, if your salary is the biggest single part of the budget, the budget can get balanced on your back. Yet it can be a principled and appropriate decision to move to a reduced position. If you chronically work more hours than you are paid for, you are probably overfunctioning. The clergy leader needs to be clear on what he or she will and won't do: "If the church decides to make this position three-quarter time, I will have to look for another position because I have to support my family." Or, "If you reduce my income, I will have to get outside supplemental employment and that will take away time from my ministry here." One recommendation: Be clear that you will not work full-time for less than a full-time salary. Any reduction in pay needs to be met with a corresponding reduction in hours. (This, of course, requires discipline from the pastor to carry out.)

Finally, a third challenge is to remember that ultimately your congregation's future is not in your hands, nor is your future in theirs. The more you can let go of the outcome in these difficult conversations, the better. Who you are is not dependent on them. There are real spiritual questions here about where your identity comes from and how you trust in God when the future is uncertain. You may very well be quite anxious for yourself. Your job is to manage your own anxiety, which may seem like an unpaid full-time job. It is not to manage theirs. You can challenge them, ask questions, hand the anxiety back to them. This last is the most important, and the hardest. Be clear on what belongs to you and what to them. Remind yourself of some basic questions to help move you to keep reflecting: "Why am I here? What is my purpose in this place at this time? What do I think? What do I want?" You will find yourself calmer when you can do this, and when you stay calm, it will be easier for others to hear you when you say what you think and what you want.

◆ *What if the leadership refuses to undertake a needed capital campaign?*
Take the long view. Many big shifts in congregational life take at least five years. Remember, any decision can be revisited. In the current discussion or any future one about a capital funds drive, define yourself clearly, without trying to convince others. "I'd like to see us take on a capital campaign, either now or in the near future. I think refurbishing the building will help make us more attractive to newcomers." Then be quiet and listen.

Even if you strongly want the campaign, don't take their "no" personally. There are any number of forces at work when boards say no to leaders, especially about money. It could be a sign that you are on the right track with your leadership direction, and that this is one way the resistance is showing up. Rather than withdrawing your leadership energy, focus on connection. Concentrate on something about the ministry you can get excited about and spend your time there. Then revisit the capital campaign matter in another year or two. If you consistently work on stewardship education over the years, you may find that leaders are in a different place in time. Growing givers may even lead to people initiating capital gifts, as they discover the joy of giving.

◆ *What if we have a conflict about giving money away versus spending it on ourselves? We have plenty of money, but we can't agree on how to spend it.*
Clergy often get caught in a triangle with those who want to give money away and those who do not. Most often the clergy leader wants the church to give more, if possible. Try not to

spend a lot of time talking with people who agree with you about "those people" who disagree, whether they are the congregation as a whole or individuals within it, since this only intensifies the triangle you are in. In addition, it perpetuates an individual model which blames others rather than looking at the church system as a whole. You can be emotionally neutral in a triangle like this while still having an opinion about the issue at hand. Continue to relate to those who disagree. Be clear in your own mind about your own view of the issue as well as how the decision will be made. Recognize that no decision is the end of the world, even one you disagree with strongly. Sometimes in this situation, the clergy are also involved in a triangle with the congregation and the denomination, especially if the external money includes denominational mission or assessments.

Church members can have a critical role to play in this conversation. One Baptist church was ready to slash its mission giving, as well as funds for education, a long-standing value in that congregation. A member of the church asked the pastor before the annual meeting if it was all right if she spoke up (not a typical action for her). At the meeting, this member clearly spoke about the fact that she did not want to be part of a church which wasn't willing to share its resources with others. The congregation voted to amend the proposed budget to restore the funds. They still had a budget gap to deal with, but they continued to live out of their professed values. This story does not mean you should anxiously recruit people to speak to support your point of view. You can, however, look for those who can calmly state what they think without accusing others (even if they disagree with you on the issue).

◆ *We can never seem to get accurate reports about money, no matter who is treasurer. Our current treasurer is an accountant, and we still can't obtain clear information.*
Financial reporting is never simply about the information involved. Remember that anxiety is like static: it makes communication difficult. For instance, you know that when you go in for a medical appointment, it can be hard to remember what the doctor said. In the same way that anxiety about your health

makes it hard to take in information, communication about money is also anxiety-ridden. Money may be a particularly high-octane topic in your church (true of most churches, but some seem to have an extra dose). You may or may not track down the historical roots of this, although you can do a little research. In addition, you can stay calm and work with the treasurer, and perhaps the congregation or council president or moderator if you have one.

Here are three ways to work on the problem: First, *define yourself*: "I'd like to work on improving our financial reporting this year." Keep thinking through what you want, and say it out loud to the parties involved. Second, *manage your own frustration level*. If you are frustrated—itself an anxious response—it will simply get in the way of the outcome you want (better reports). Third, *try to simply get curious about the situation,* and see what you can learn about yourself, the treasurer, and money in this church system. Expect this problem to take some time to get better. Remember that changing personnel does not change emotional process. As the question notes, it does not seem to matter who is the treasurer. Still, keep your eye out for a calm, mature person to recruit to be the next treasurer.

◆ *How do we improve our meetings about money? They last too long and we can never seem to make a decision.*
Here are some questions to ask before and during every meeting about money:

- ◆ What is the purpose of this meeting?
- ◆ What are my goals for myself in this meeting?
- ◆ What is the financial question that needs to be decided, and by when?
- ◆ Who else needs to contribute to this decision? Are we getting enough outside input, without avoiding our responsibility as leaders?
- ◆ Are we appropriately balancing the financial needs in the present with the needs of the future? What are we hoping will be true in ten years? Thirty?

◆ Are we clear on the roles each person and group is playing—pastor, treasurer, governing board, finance committee, congregation—and what each one's responsibility is?

◆ On what assumptions are we basing our financial decisions? How do we know they are accurate?

◆ How are our values and our faith informing this decision about money?

Meetings with this clarity, whether it is the trustees, finance committee, vestry/council, or budget committee, will lead to better decisions. Say out loud, or coach the chairperson to say: "The purpose of this meeting is _____. Our hope for tonight is that by the end of the meeting we will _____ (generate budget options, make a decision on staffing, be ready for the church annual meeting). We intend to finish by _____." You may not get as far as you wanted or finish quite on time, but you will get farther and finish earlier than if you have an unclear, open-ended meeting. At the end of every meeting, take a few minutes to assess: How did we do? How could we improve for the next meeting?

Murray Bowen used to say you only have to be the least anxious person in the room. In most meetings where budget is an issue, or where a big decision about money has to be made, being the least anxious person present is not that hard—other people are typically fairly anxious. You only have to step your own anxiety about money down a bit to make a big difference for yourself and for those around you. Stay relatively light about how the meeting goes, and let go of any particular outcome. While clear intentions do help meetings go better, you can never completely control other people. And the more you want to, the more they resist. You might try mentally walking the line between serious and humorous to help yourself stay on your toes.

◆ *What if the biggest employer in town closes?*
A major community change like this requires a thoughtful response from congregational leaders. It's always important to recognize that we are part of larger systems. Even if your church

has few or no people working for that company, your church will feel the impact. Anxiety in the wider community touches all the systems within it. First, if you do have people affected by this closure, make sure you give people permission to adjust their giving to fit their circumstances, without guilt. And of course, this is not just about the money. If people lose their jobs, there's a huge emotional impact, especially if they were employed a long time. As when a substantial giver dies, you need to have conversations with the church leadership on possible budget implications and what the options are for addressing it. In addition, don't hesitate to offer other members the challenge of stepping up their giving as they are able. You can do this in a way that is gracious, open, and not willful. Finally, you do not need to assume this is a long-term disaster for the community. When Fort Devens, an Army base in Ayer, Massachusetts, closed in the 1990s, the community ultimately found that the result was a more diverse and stable local economy, which benefited the churches as well as residents. Reverend Phil Goff, pastor of the Federated Church of Ayer at the time, immediately engaged with community leaders to help craft the best solution for the three towns involved, as well as for the church. No matter what the ultimate impact of this event, avoiding panic will help you and other leaders think creatively about how best to respond in the present.

◆ *We are facing a big deficit as we approach the end of the year. What should we do? We are in crisis mode.*
First, take a deep breath and step back from the immediate worries. Think through the factors that may be at play. Practically speaking, almost all congregations do not receive giving in twelve equal portions. Long-time Baptist pastor Joe Kutter says, "When I made a point of learning the history of both giving and spending, my anxiety was seriously reduced. Expenses were frequently front-loaded in the winter and income was back-loaded between Christmas and the first of the new year. We had a deficit eleven months a year." Start by reviewing at least three years of giving patterns to see what happens in your particular church.

If there is a real crisis with an abnormal income–expense gap, a critical question is, "Why now?" Sometimes the apparent cause of a church financial crisis is external, sometimes internal. In the financial meltdown of 2008–2009, of course, churches experienced a significant external impact, from dramatically reduced endowment income to church members losing jobs and cutting their giving. And the overall climate around stewardship and budgeting was affected by the high anxiety the financial crisis generated. These effects are ongoing.

In addition, internal congregational dynamics can affect giving in significant ways. For example, when leaders step out in faith, income may show a big dip, at least for a time, as the system reacts to the upset in the balance. As we have seen, all churches have some kind of financial and emotional balance or homeostasis, and strong moves by leaders upset that balance. The congregation or parts of the congregation may say, in effect, "change back," and sometimes this demand shows up in giving patterns. It may be explicit ("If you don't stop this second worship service, I'm going to cancel my pledge") or more subtle, with an unexpected and unexplained dip in giving. Typically, if leaders can stay on track in a way that is principled but not rigid, people will calm down, and giving will rebound. When you are not sure you can pay the bills, it takes some fortitude to stay the course. Of course, as we have seen, other internal factors can be at work: a significant death, changing demographic patterns in the congregation, or an unexpected capital expense.

Whatever the cause or apparent cause, leaders wonder, "How do we pay our bills?" In a church financial crisis, it is not the bottom-line deficit that makes the difference, but the resourcefulness of the leadership. Ask leaders to consider not only the dollars, but also their own principles and their own point of view. Review previously agreed-upon principles in the life of the congregation or in your particular tradition. Do anything you can do to get yourself and others out of crisis mode and into thoughtful reflection. Some ways to do this are:

◆ humor (seriousness is a sign of anxiety);

◆ reflection on a Scripture passage;

◆ individual time to think (even in the middle of a meeting);

◆ practice in defining self ("I statements" that are true self-definition, not "I think you should...");

◆ telling stories about past financial challenges that were met.

All of these practices can help people quit simply reacting, and start thinking about the bigger picture. Bob Hunter suggests, "We're more likely to weather a whitewater period in our congregation if we take a deep breath, which means use the oxygen that's available to us, and in a clear way then focus again on vision. What is our purpose for being here? And, here's how we will continue to function as a congregation here."[4] Coming through a financial crisis well does not mean that your budget will automatically remain the same. Sometimes difficult decisions have to be made. Still, remember to celebrate the positives along the way, and again when you are on the other side. Focus on the congregation's strengths, resourcefulness, and generosity. Thank leaders who have given extra time and money in response to the challenge.

◆ *What if we have one influential member (and substantial giver) who wants to control all the money decisions?*
No leader can challenge a controlling member alone. Whether you are the clergy leader or a layperson, you have to have allies. You must be prepared to take the consequences—conflict in the congregation and/or the individual removing his or her pledge to the church. If you and other leaders can stay relatively calm and clear, it's possible that the member will not actually quit giving, but there are no guarantees. This is a good reason for recruiting mature people for key leadership spots, so they can have the necessary courage at important decision points. While there may be times to thoughtfully discuss with leaders how to take a stand, try not to complain about this person to others. Instead, work on your own relationship with this individual, rather than avoiding him or her. Stay in touch, but don't talk about money or even church all the time. Pay attention to him or her pas-

torally. If you feel emotionally spooked by this person, get some coaching. Remember, the people who set us off most at church reflect something in our family story. You can continue to work on your own reactivity.

When the time comes to take a stand, do it in a clear and calm manner, in partnership with other key leaders: "Frank, the trustees have decided to make a different decision about our investments, and I agree with their decision." Coach the congregation president (or equivalent) to stay calm as well. If Frank repeats his threat to pull his pledge, you can say, "I'll be sorry to see that happen, but you have to make your own decisions about giving." After the fact, continue to stay in touch, without anxiously pursuing Frank. In situations like this, sometimes the controller settles down when leaders are clear, and sometimes not.

◆ *We have quite a few new members, but they can't/don't give as much as the older (in age and tenure) members, who are gradually dying. What should we do?*
This is a common issue which does not have a quick fix. However, here are three ways to work on it over time. First, develop a comprehensive personal finance and stewardship education program. Remember, you cannot assume that people know anything about giving, even if they grew up in church. Second, be sure you are clear about vision and direction. Those who are younger, as we have discussed, will be less likely to give out of habit or duty; institutional loyalty is not automatic for them. They want to give to causes they believe in. Finally, be clear about what you want from people, and don't hesitate to ask them. Be specific about what you are asking for and why. This includes asking older members for planned gifts so they can continue to help support ministry even after they are gone, as well as asking younger members to begin to give and to increase their giving over time.

IDEAS TO PONDER

No matter what specific financial challenges you face in your church, let me remind you of some constants we have discussed that you can pay attention to as you move forward. Each of us does have control over certain matters in our own setting. Even if you can't conjure money out of the air, you can keep yourself on track with your own ministry, and help others do the same. Leadership does make a difference, even—or perhaps most of all—when times are difficult. Here are three fundamental ideas to remember.

First, *pay attention to your own anxiety.* Anxious leaders cannot see options. If you can manage yourself, you leave room for creativity (your own and others') to emerge. You will be able to better navigate the challenges if you are calmer. Jeffrey Miller puts it this way: "If fear is contagious, then so is courage. In an anxious organization, a single individual can have a powerful and wide-ranging effect just by mastering his or her own anxiety."[5] How do you do that? "Mastering" anxiety may be a tall order under the pressures of a budget crisis. Still, you can bring it down a notch. Maintain your spiritual life. Remember that it is not all up to you. Finally, keep your sense of humor.

Second, *clarify who is responsible for what.* Leadership comes with responsibility, and the financial support of the ministry is a big part of this. At the same time, in a church, decision-making needs to be shared appropriately. Don't carry the group on your back, because over time it will break you and cripple them. Insist that the leadership share information with the people as a whole, as a way of sharing the responsibility with the whole congregation.

Third, *keep your focus on vision.* When money is tight, it's easy to lose sight of the bigger picture. Keep working on your own clarity. If you are not clear, it will be hard for others around you to be clear. Do a little bit of thinking about this every day. Even two minutes, every day, can be enough. Ask yourself, "Why am I here? What am I called to do? What might we be called to do together?" Focusing on vision does not mean ignoring fiscal realities. The question at times may be, "Given our resources, what might we do?" Ministry needs resources, yet even unlimited resources are useless without vision—you and others need to know what the money is for. If you are a staff person or lay leader, focus on doing your job well and leading with intention in your area of responsibility. Get feedback from the leader about what he or she is after. And ask yourself the same questions: "Why am I here? What am I called to do? What might we be called to do together?"

◆ *Questions*
Here are six additional questions to ask yourself as you face the inevitable money challenges in your church.

1. How is this an opportunity for you to grow?

2. What is your responsibility, and what is not?

3. How might you draw on your faith resources to help you and your church with this challenge?

4. What do you want?

5. What's the worst that could happen? Can you handle that?

6. For what are you grateful in this situation? What can you celebrate?

chapter seven

Pray About the Money

Clearly, the purpose of wealth is not security. The purpose of wealth is reckless generosity, the kind that sings of the lavish love of God, the kind that rekindles hope on dark days, the kind that reminds us that God is with us always. It creates in the holy heart a freedom of spirit that takes a person light-footed through the world, scattering possibility as it goes.

— Joan Chittister and Rowan Williams, *Uncommon Gratitude*[1]

THIS CHAPTER COULD be the first as easily as the last. Our relationship with money is, ultimately, a spiritual matter. We can begin and end all of our considerations of money with prayer.

GIVE THANKS

One of the best ways to shift our relationship with money is through the spiritual practice of gratitude. Our society is very good at noticing what we do not have. The advertising industry makes it their business to make us think we are deprived if we don't buy what they're selling. The economic crunch means some of us have less than we used to, as individuals and institutions, and we notice that. The media in general tries to raise anxiety, not foster contentment, let alone celebration. Yet we can make different choices about how we relate to our resources, beginning with gratitude and celebration.

Lately, I have been attempting to cultivate celebration as a spiritual practice. I must confess it does not come naturally. It is much easier for me to notice what isn't happening! Yet life becomes much more enjoyable when I can focus on what I *have* rather than what I do *not* have. I have more energy and motivation to pursue the things that are important to me when I am celebrating than when I am bemoaning. For example, recently I had to drive two hours to a preaching engagement. It poured rain the whole trip. While I was whining to myself, I suddenly realized: I have a car around me! I'm not out in the rain. I am blessed by owning a car to drive. My experience of the rest of the drive was quite different.

In church life, a focus on celebration and abundance begins with the leader. What kind of spiritual practice do you have? What's the harvest you see in your life and in your church? Can you notice even the smallest signs of hope and possibility, and rejoice? When you look, you may see more than you think—beginning with Scripture. Walter Brueggemann suggests, "The Bible starts out with a liturgy of abundance. Genesis 1 is a song of praise for God's generosity.... In an orgy of fruitfulness, everything in its kind is to multiply to overflowing goodness that pours from God's creator spirit."[2]

David, a Methodist minister, found that when he decided to go back to a basic prayer life in his ministry, that alone helped him to relate differently to the church finances. He simply went to the worship space every morning and sat there for five minutes. It wasn't much, he knew, but he had spent so many years working away at his ministry, especially the financial and administrative side, without enough spiritual support, so he figured anything would help. He intentionally prayed about the church's finances and asked for the ability to let go. He noticed a change almost immediately, and over time, he found that he was able to be quite different in church council meetings during the financial reports. Instead of steeling himself, he began by saying, "I'd like us to start this meeting with a period of giving thanks." The hard-headed business people looked at him with a shock the first meeting he did this. He made a little joke of it, "I'm the minister, after all. I decided it was my job to make us do this."

They chuckled, and then they went along with it. Rather than the perfunctory opening prayer, after a while people began to share genuine thanksgivings. He found that he experienced himself as both lighter and more grounded in those meetings. There were still sharp disagreements at moments as they faced the seemingly endless ups and downs in their financial life. Others still looked to him as the savior. Still, he was more able to let go than he had ever been before. And the tone of the meetings shifted in a more positive direction. People had a greater sense of hope and possibility.

A life of gratitude and prayer does not mean you will get all the money you want or think you need, personally and institutionally. Yet you will experience more grace, more trust, and more celebration for what you do have. You will relate to your own resources and your church's resources with increasing freedom, whether you have a lot or a little. The spiritual can come to influence the practical, as you are present in your leadership role in a different way.

You can begin to view money as a gift of God, rather than something that is frightening or dangerous. Relating to money then becomes an opportunity for spiritual growth. Adele Azar-Rucquoi, in her thoughtful book *Money as Sacrament,* describes her experience of moving from a childhood in a family grocery business, to life as a Roman Catholic nun, to leaving the convent and living with very limited resources, to receiving a substantial inheritance from her parents. She says, "All money is manna. Strictly speaking it is in no way earned, as we like to believe, but it is given to us as world citizens, necessary for our nourishment." She adds, "Like prayer, money is everywhere, linking us with one another and bringing something new."[3]

In addition to incorporating your financial life into your prayer life, how can you incorporate your prayer life into your financial life? One of Azar-Rucquoi's recommendations is to pay more attention to the flow of money into and out of your life. For example, she suggests you light a candle when you pay your bills.[4] Her perspective caused me to be more aware of how the money I spend helps support other families. I can be grateful for the ways my resources have the opportunity to help others—

through my giving, of course, but also through my spending. I can be aware of where the money I spend goes. When I get my hair cut, I am helping my hairdresser's family. When I leave a more generous tip in a café or hotel room, I am making a contribution to the life of someone who has served me. Even more anonymous purchases help pay someone's salary.

In addition, when you view money as a gift and remember that it is far from ultimate, you can shift your perspective at church as well as in your daily financial life. During the finance committee meeting or a conversation with the treasurer, see if you can step back. Can you think about God's gift of money in the moment of the meeting or the conversation? What difference does it make if you do? Set some spiritual experiments for yourself. If you are dreading the next meeting about money, spend five minutes in gratitude beforehand. Or pray after the meeting instead of rehashing it in your mind. Read Matthew 6 before or after—or read it aloud to start the meeting. Or bring an object to remind you of God and place it on the table during the meeting. What are your own ideas to frame the business of the church as a gift rather than a burden, so you might experience more peace while doing that business?

EMBODY YOUR PRAYER

Spiritual life includes our bodies. As we have seen, money is so closely linked with survival that we can easily experience a fight-or-flight physical reaction in our relationship with money. How many times have you noticed your heart pounding in a budget meeting, for example? Or have you ever felt short of breath when you sit down to pay the bills which are bigger than you expected? An experience of unexpected abundance can also produce a physical reaction: when you receive a windfall, you may want to jump for joy.

Here are three ways to begin to bring your physical life into your prayer about money. First of all, simply see if you can begin to notice when and how your body reacts when money is under discussion. Does your heart speed up when a certain individual attends the budget meeting? Do you sweat more before your stewardship sermon? There's nothing negative about these reactions—they are perfectly normal. Yet becoming a student of your own reactions can help you have more choices as you respond, and give you space and time to pray rather than simply react.

Second, try some kind of spiritual practice that incorporates something to do with your body. Try meditative prayer, where you watch your breathing as you pray.[5] Or practice meditation while you walk. I know a number of clergy who incorporate their spiritual practice into their running—or even their knitting. What can you do that helps you to be in your body more, as a spiritual practice? How can you be aware of your body while you pray, rather than using your mind only? Over time, the practice of some type of mindful prayer can help you become calmer and more at peace with money matters.

Third, bodily awareness does not have to be limited to designated prayer sessions. In the moment, in meetings and conversations about money, you can be more aware of your body. Notice your breath right now as you read, and remember that God is as close to you as your breath. Try to do the same when you are in a meeting. It takes practice to come back to this awareness, especially in a difficult meeting, yet even a moment's awareness can change your presence in that meeting. You can ground yourself in your body by noticing the floor under your feet, as the budget reports are handed out in the middle of the meeting. When someone is talking and you notice yourself getting anxious, try putting your hands on the table to feel its surface. It only takes a moment, and no one need know what you are doing.

Spiritual practice has that name for a reason—it takes practice. And the fear that quickly lodges in our body when money is under discussion is a powerful force. But over time (years of time), you can become more aware and less at the mercy of your own reactivity. And you can be more aware of God's presence with you every moment.

✓

Tips for Incorporating a Spiritual Approach into Your Life with Money and into Your Leadership Around Money

1

Find a way to connect your spiritual life with your personal financial life. Integrating your life in this way will help you lead more effectively around money.

2

Read Scripture about money devotionally. Pick a passage such as Matthew 6:25 ("Do not worry about your life...") and use a practice such as *lectio divina* (meditative reading of Scripture).[6]

3

Practice noticing your reactive responses around money (fear, wanting, envy). Don't try to change them, simply notice. Over time (a long time) this practice can deeply affect you for the better.

4

Pray for members of your congregation who are struggling financially. One effect of offering their names to God is to help you gain clarity about what you can and cannot do to help. It can also help you let go of any judgmental attitudes you may have.

5

Pray for members of your congregation who have ample resources. This can help you let go of any judgmental attitudes you may have toward them.

6

Pray for members of your congregation who have a different view of
how to handle the congregation's resources. This can help you let go of
any judgmental attitudes you may have toward them,
and will help you work more productively with them.

7

Make a list of five things you are thankful for daily. This practice will
help you focus on what you have, not what you do not have.

DISCOVER YOUR SELF-WORTH

We all have a story around money, a unique relationship with
it. And God wants us to find our true self—in relation to money
and everything else. Our true self is a self that is dependent only
on God for our understanding of who we are, not on our possessions or our salary, or our success in stewardship or our ministry as a whole. All those, when we take our cue from them,
are expressions of false or pseudo-self. Everyone lives out of this
false self to some degree. But the more we live out of our de-
pendence on God, the freer we will be in all aspects of life, including our leadership in congregational life—and our financial
life.

Ask yourself this question: "Do I think my worth depends on
my success, on how successful the stewardship campaign is, and
how successful my church is?" Many clergy were either the oldest child or the one on whom expectations fell heavily in the
family. We are prone to the temptation of finding our value in
what we produce. It is a long spiritual process to truly accept in
the depths of our being that God loves us no matter how much
money people give, or how much we make. And of course, we
are tempted by the trappings of success in other areas, too, particularly how many people are in the pews each week.

If your sense of yourself depends on success, especially financial success, and not on your ultimate acceptance by God, you
are living on shaky spiritual ground. You can easily find your

feet knocked from under you by the inevitable setbacks in congregational life. It is critical that you address these matters for yourself, whether through prayer, spiritual direction, or therapy (or all of the above). Spending this time is not selfish. As you live more deeply into your full acceptance by God, it is good for you, good for your family, and good for your church. You will lead from a place of greater spiritual calm and depth. And you will be able to lead more effectively in the area of money, because you will have money in its proper perspective. Money is always secondary, never ultimate.

You can celebrate when you do see good things happening at church, and you should! Yet, when you are emotionally and spiritually dependent on those good things, you have spiritual work to do. As a responsible eldest daughter I have to work on this every day. I know in my heart of hearts my first response is to think I have to earn my salvation by producing. The practice of living out of gratitude helps me overcome that profound sense that it is all up to me. Letting go of ultimate responsibility for the financial life of the church you lead is truly a deeply spiritual matter. You cannot delegate leadership, yet you can delegate anxiety—"downward" to those you lead, and also, and more importantly, "upward" to God. You still have key responsibilities in this area, of course. But the practice of letting go positions you differently in relationship to the challenges. You can recognize the outcome is not up to you.

One minister decided to begin a practice of checking in twice a day to see if she had been experiencing that sense of God's gracious provision, rather than anxious obligation. She was astonished to find how often her thoughts flew to obligation and fear, especially in the area of money. But simply checking in this way each day over time helped her move toward greater awareness of God's love and provision for her. She found herself less anxious, less critical of others—and herself—and more able to live out of joy and gratitude.

The process of growing a sense of self apart from what you produce includes a deep acceptance of where you are in your journey, just as God accepts you where you are. You can celebrate the small steps you are able to take along the way. You have anxiety about money? Well, money and your response to it can be your teachers. You had an emotional crash after the church denied you a raise yet again? Remember, that's normal—and then ask, what can you learn from this experience? Can you receive God's love even though you feel like the church doesn't love you enough or that you aren't doing a good enough job, and despite your expectation that there would be enough money for a raise? God accepts you as you are, and God wants you to be free in relation to money. Both are true. Be patient with yourself: you have a lifetime to walk through, where you will encounter these issues again and again. Like our parishioners, we deal with money every day. Through the years, we will find many opportunities to practice living out of freedom in financial affairs.

INVITE OTHERS TO PRAY

A spiritual focus for our financial life goes beyond our individual spirituality to life together in community. If together we can act on our spiritual principles rather than out of fear and anxiety, we will be less stressed as a church, and will make better decisions. While you can only focus on yourself and your functioning, you can invite others to join you in moving toward a spiritual perspective on money. You cannot make people pray about money or anything else, but you can invite them on a journey of celebration, and you can begin to create a space where gratitude is the first word.

One Episcopal priest's shift in his spiritual life enabled him to be different in his leadership. In particular, he found himself noticing people he might not have thought of for leadership who were also tuned in spiritually. The vestry—and even the finance committee—slowly became more comfortable with conversation about stewardship and the budget from a faith perspective. If we can together act on our principles rather than out of fear and anxiety, we will be able to make different decisions. If we seek to be thoughtful and not reactive, we will make different decisions. If clergy and key lay leaders are able, out of spiritual power, to stick to the plan in the face of the reactivity of others, churches will be healthier and more resilient places, even in the face of high anxiety, global recession, and changing institutional realities.

It is not easy to live this way. The pressures to be too busy for prayer and spiritual practice, individually and at meetings, are enormous: "Our agenda is just too full!" But if we provide this element of leadership, our own lives will be transformed and our communities will become different. And the decisions we make about money and about other matters will be much easier. If you are praying, your relationship with money will be different, and you will relate to others differently—less haranguing, less judgmental, less anxious. You will be more open, more accepting, more able to be light about the challenges and about the quirks of the people you lead. A key spiritual endeavor is to accept those who have a different point of view on church finances. It is all too easy to view those who disagree with judgment, frustration, even anger when they appear to be roadblocks in the way to ministry. When you roll your eyes, complain about others, and inwardly resent them, you are getting in the way of your own spiritual growth—and theirs. Pray for them, open your heart to them, spend time with them. And you may be surprised what happens over the years.

If you had to make a choice between teaching your people about stewardship and teaching them about prayer, I'd say teach them about prayer. This is a false dichotomy, of course. But if people are serious about prayer over time, their relationship with money will change. And remember that we can learn from our people as well. My first year in pastoral ministry, we faced a shortfall as we approached the end of the year. What to do? Sitting around the table with the executive board, I could feel my anxiety rising. Was it me and my leadership? As we continued the conversation, the treasurer said at last, "We'll just have to pray about it." I remember thinking, if the *treasurer* thinks it's a spiritual matter, we're probably going to be okay. We were, and we continued to be for the next twelve years of my ministry in that church. I did learn, however, that the December crunch was typical—and I learned to be a little less anxious in December each year.

Now, you cannot make your people pray about money or anything else. Family systems thinking suggests that you work with people who are motivated, rather than trying to chase after and "motivate" people who are not. Look for other leaders in the congregation who are interested in spiritual matters, and teach them more about prayer. Then look for people who are involved with the money who have a hint of interest in spiritual matters, and work with them. Over time—and I mean over the years—more people will come along. Your best "prospects" for this kind of work are people who are calmer. Teach them to pray, and recruit them for leadership positions.

Cynthia Maybeck tells about her time as pastor of Trinity Church in Northboro, Massachusetts. She recalls one lay leader who was a banker by profession. "We were talking about risking a huge deficit budget for the purpose of hiring an additional clergy member, and he said, 'You know, Monday through Friday I work to avoid risk, and at church meetings we keep talking about taking risks for the sake of the gospel. And I'm starting to think it's kind of fun!' And when he said that he had laughter in his eyes as well as in his voice."[7] Maybeck has found it a blessing in her ministry to be able to teach people the spirituality of abundance and see how that affects their way of thinking about money.

Maybeck also tells about another woman who took part in the church's involvement with a ministry to the homeless. At a worship service, she heard a testimony from a man who gave thanks because he found a quarter and could buy a Dunkin Donuts munchkin and use the restroom as a paying customer. When she went through the Dunkin Donuts drive-through the next day, she was in tears of gratitude for all that she had. Her experience of the church's mission changed her relationship with her own resources.[8] Prayer and action for ministry go hand in hand. Pray and take action, together founded in your life of prayer, then see how your spiritual life is affected by your actions. In this way you will be able to manage your money together and spend it for ministry with more grace, more trust, more celebration for what you do have.

Clergy and church leaders who make choices grounded in prayer and their own faith will lead churches that are healthier and more resilient. Even in the face of high anxiety, changing institutional realities and global recession, they will do better institutionally—and spiritually. Quality administration and deep spiritual practice can walk hand in hand to help institutions thrive. When you have this kind of spiritual leadership in place, your congregation overall will be a calmer place. You and your leaders will be able to say, "We can handle this," as the inevitable financial ups and downs come. You will be able to deal with differing points of view about what to do with a surplus or what to do with a deficit. You will be able to make decisions out of a sense of God's provision in good times and in bad. You will be able to make hard decisions, knowing it is not the end of the world. You will be able to celebrate all that God has done, is doing, and will do in your unique life together.

TAKE AN INFINITE VIEW OF MONEY

Finally, we need to learn to place money in its proper perspective, to view money from the perspective of infinity, rather than the anxious, limited perspective it is so easy to have. James Carse begins his book *Finite and Infinite Games* with these words: "There are at least two kinds of games. One could be called finite, the other infinite. A finite game is played for the purpose of winning, an infinite game for the purpose of continuing the play.... Finite players play within boundaries; infinite players play with boundaries.... Surprise causes finite play to end; it is the reason for infinite play to continue."[9]

Money is the ultimate finite game; we human beings have made it up and agreed to follow the rules. And we have all thought there is not enough—we have experienced scarcity. But we can choose a different view. We are in fact in a different game, in God's infinite game. We do not have to allow limited funds or our fears that there won't be enough in the future to define our view of ourselves or of our ministries. Scarcity is a finite game. God's way is an infinite game, the abundant offering of God's grace to us.

This is what I want for you—for clergy, for lay leaders, and for the church: to have an infinite view of your relationship with your resources. To experience astounding gratitude, to live with a sense of wonder for the amazing thing that is your life. To be in awareness of God and God's provision moment by moment. For your business meetings about money to have an element of prayer that is not perfunctory, but real. To worry less and celebrate more, and to be clear on what you want for yourself and for your church. May we all be surprised by God as we take this journey together.

IDEAS TO PONDER

Go forth and save, spend, give, count, manage, do all that you need to do with the money that is yours and that is the church's, with courage, forethought, freedom, skill, generosity, and care. Do all this in the name of Jesus Christ, who went before, who calls us and makes it possible for us to do the ministry that we have.

◆ Questions

Here are six questions to consider as you engage spiritually with money matters, personally and at church.

1. How have you experienced God's provision?

2. What causes you to be distracted by anxieties about scarcity?

3. How can you incorporate your money life into your prayer life, and your prayer life into your money life?

4. How can you bring your spiritual leadership at church into the area of money?

5. For whom do you need to pray about money?

6. For what are you most grateful?

Notes

CHAPTER 1

1. Roger Jones, "Money, Anxiety, and Abundance," *Quest* 67, no. 7 (July/August 2011): 1–2.

2. David W. Miller, "Wealth Creation as Integrated with Faith: A Protestant Reflection," a presentation at the conference *Muslim, Christian, and Jewish Views on the Creation of Wealth,* University of Notre Dame, April 23–24, 2007; http://www3.nd.edu/~ethics/wcConference/presentations.shtml.

3. Miller, "Wealth Creation as Integrated with Faith."

4. Justo L. González, *Faith and Wealth: A History of Early Christian Ideas on the Origin, Significance, and Use of Money* (San Francisco: Harper & Row, 1990), 114.

5. J. Philip Wogaman, *Christian Ethics: A Historical Introduction* (Louisville: Westminster John Knox Press, 1993), 62.

6. John Calvin, *Institutes,* Book III, chapter 10.

7. Joan Chittister, *The Rule of Benedict: Insights for the Ages* (New York: Crossroad, 1996), 107.

8. Quoted in Katherine D'Arcy Blanchard, "'If you do not do this you are not now a Christian': Martin Luther's Pastoral Teachings on Money," *Word and World* 26, no. 3 (Summer 2006): 302.

9. Barbara Owen, "Love, Money and Pigs," *The Lutheran* (September 1996): 11.

10. Barbara Owen, ed., *Jesus, Remember Me: Words of Assurance from Martin Luther* (Minneapolis: Augsburg Fortress, 1998), 80.

11. John Wesley, "The Use of Money," Sermon 50, quoted from the 1872 edition, ed. Thomas Jackson; http://www.umcmission.org/Find-Resources/John-Wesley-Sermons/Sermon-50-The-Use-of-Money.

CHAPTER 2
1. Bob Hunter, interview by Margaret Marcuson, Leadership Adventure Teleconference, "How Do You Get Clear about Stewardship?" February 25, 2010.

CHAPTER 3
1. Howard Anderson, interview by Margaret Marcuson, Leadership Adventure Teleconference, "How to Ask People to Give More Money to Church," September 29, 2011.

2. M. Douglas Meeks, *God the Economist* (Minneapolis: Fortress Press, 1989), 75.

3. Hunter interview.

4. J. Clif Christopher, *Not Your Parents' Offering Plate: A New Vision for Financial Stewardship* (Nashville: Abingdon Press, 2008), 13. Third is the fiscal responsibility of the institution.

5. Christian Smith, Michael O. Emerson, and Patricia Snell, *Passing the Plate: Why American Christians Don't Give Away More Money* (New York: Oxford University Press, 2008), 140–142, 179–180.

6. Joseph Clifford, interview by Margaret Marcuson, Leadership Adventure Teleconference, "Do You Know Your Church's Money Story?" March 24, 2010.

7. Jonathan Eric Carroll, interview by Margaret Marcuson, Leadership Adventure Teleconference, "How Do You Preach about Money?" May 26, 2011.

8. James Lamkin, interview by Margaret Marcuson, Leadership Adventure Teleconference, "How Do We Manage Ourselves around Money at Church?" January 27, 2011.

9. Anderson interview.

10. Piet Levy, "Report Says Tithing And Church Spending Hit Record Lows," *Huffington Post,* October 13, 2011; http://www.huffingtonpost.com/2011/10/13/state-of-church-giving_n_1009948.html.

11. *Giving USA 2012: The Annual Report on Philanthropy for the Year 2011: Executive Summary,* Center on Philanthropy at Indiana University, 18; http://store.givingusareports.org/2012-Giving-USA-The-Annual-Report-on-Philanthropy-for-the-Year-2011-Executive-Summary-P43.aspx.

12. Christopher, *Not Your Parents' Offering Plate,* ix.

13. Hunter interview.

14. The Lake Institute on Faith and Giving's "2013 Congregational Economic Impact Study" has some helpful analysis and suggestions for church leaders; http://philanthropy.iupui.edu/congregational-economic-impact-study.

15. Israel Galindo, interview by Margaret Marcuson, Leadership Adventure Teleconference, "What Is Your Responsibility for Church Finance?" February 24, 2011.

CHAPTER 4
1. Margaret Bendroth, "The Past Isn't Past: The Weight of Congregational History," *The Christian Century* 127 (February 9, 2010): 30–32.

2. Kathy Wiseman, interview by Margaret Marcuson, Leadership Adventure Teleconference, "What's a Leader to Do about Money at Church?" December 9, 2010.

3. Lamkin interview.

CHAPTER 5
1. Galindo interview.

2. William Enright, interview by Margaret Marcuson, Leadership Adventure Teleconference, "How Can You Make It Easier to Talk about Money at Church?" October 27, 2011.

3. Enright interview.

4. One helpful book is Israel Galindo, Elaine Boomer, and Don Reagan, *A Family Genogram Workbook* (Richmond, Va.: Educational Consultants, 2006). A free study guide is available from their website, http://www.israel-galindo.com. An online resource for creating a computerized genogram is GenoPro, www.genopro.com.

5. Galindo interview.

6. Ed Bacon, interview by Margaret Marcuson, Leadership Adventure Teleconference, "How Do Church Leaders Face a Financial Crisis?" October 28, 2010.

7. Bacon interview.

8. James E. Hughes, Jr., *Family Wealth: Keeping It in the Family* (New York: Bloomberg Press, 2004), 17.

CHAPTER 6
1. Hunter interview.

2. See the delightful illustrated version of this story by Patricia C. McKissack, *Flossie and the Fox* (New York: Dial Books for Young Readers, 1986).

3. Hunter interview.

4. Hunter interview.

5. Jeffrey A. Miller, *The Anxious Organization: Why Smart Companies Do Dumb Things* (Tempe, Az.: Facts on Demand Press, 2008), 85.

CHAPTER 7
1. Joan Chittister and Rowan Williams, *Uncommon Gratitude: Alleluia for All That Is* (Collegeville, Minn.: Liturgical Press, 2010), 22.

2. Walter Brueggemann, "The Liturgy of Abundance, The Myth of Scarcity," *The Christian Century* 116, no. 10 (March 24, 1999): 342–249.

3. Adele Azar-Rucquoi, *Money as Sacrament: Finding the Sacred in Money* (Berkeley, Calif.: Celestial Arts, 2002), xiv.

4. Azar-Rucquoi, *Money as Sacrament,* 214.

5. One good guide is Martin Laird, O.S.A., *Into the Silent Land: A Guide to the Christian Practice of Contemplation* (New York: Oxford University Press, 2006).

6. A couple of resources are: Lin Johnson, *Everything the Bible Says about Money* (Minneapolis: Bethany House Publishers, 2011), and Brian Kluth, *You are Invited on a 40 Day Spiritual Journey to a More Generous Life;* http://www.kluth.org/generouslife/book.pdf.

7. Cynthia Maybeck, interview by Margaret Marcuson, Leadership Adventure Teleconference, "What Does Money Have to Do with Prayer?" December 1, 2011.

8. Maybeck interview.

9. James Carse, *Finite and Infinite Games: A Vision of Life as Play and Possibility* (New York: Random House, 1986), 3, 18, 22.

Further Resources

BOOKS

Collier, Charles W. *Wealth in Families*. Cambridge, Mass.: Harvard University, 2012.

Friedman, Edwin H. *A Failure of Nerve*. New York: Seabury Press, 2007.

Friedman, Edwin H. *Generation to Generation: Family Process in Church and Synagogue*. New York: Guilford, 1985.

Galindo, Israel. *The Hidden Lives of Congregations: Understanding Congregational Dynamics*. Herndon, Va.: Alban Institute, 2004.

Galindo, Israel. *Perspectives on Congregational Leadership: Applying Systems Thinking for Effective Leadership*. Richmond, Va.: Educational Consultants, 2009.

Hotchkiss, Dan. *Ministry and Money: A Guide for Clergy and Their Friends*. Bethesda, Md.: Alban Institute, 2002.

Jamieson, Janet T., and Philip D. Jamieson. *Ministry and Money: A Practical Guide for Pastors*. Louisville, Ky.: Westminster John Knox, 2009.

Jeavons, Thomas, and Rebekah Basinger. *Growing Givers' Hearts: Treating Fundraising as Ministry.* San Francisco: Jossey-Bass, 2000.

Keucher, Gerald W. *Remember the Future: Financial Leadership and Asset Management for Congregations.* New York: Church Publishing, 2006.

Lane, Charles R. *Ask, Thank, Tell: Improving Stewardship Ministry in Your Congregation.* Minneapolis: Augsburg Fortress, 2006.

Richardson, Ronald W. *Becoming a Healthier Pastor: Family Systems Theory and the Pastor's Own Family.* Minneapolis: Fortress Press, 2005.

Richardson, Ronald W. *Creating a Healthier Church: Family Systems Theory, Leadership, and Congregational Life.* Minneapolis: Fortress Press, 1996.

Steinke, Peter L. *A Door Set Open: Grounding Change in Mission and Hope.* Herndon, Va.: Alban Institute, 2010.

Twist, Lynne, with Teresa Barker. *The Soul of Money: Reclaiming the Wealth of Our Inner Resources.* New York: W.W. Norton & Co., 2006.

WEBSITES AND BLOGS

Margaret Marcuson
www.margaretmarcuson.com
Provides my own latest thinking about money and ministry, as well as other writings on church leadership.

Bowen Center for the Study of the Family
www.thebowencenter.org/
Information about Bowen family system theory, books, audio, and video available for purchase.

Center for Stewardship Leaders at Luther Seminary
www.luthersem.edu/stewardship
Subscribe to their fine newsletter.

Design Group International's blog, *The Organizational Development Muse*
www.designgroupinternational.com/TheOrganizational DevelopmentMuse/
This excellent blog provides articles on stewardship, capital campaigns, and many aspects of organizational life.

Generous Matters
generousmatters.com/
Rebekah Basinger's thoughtful blog.

Lake Institute on Faith and Giving
www.philanthropy.iupui.edu/the-lake-institute
Ongoing research and educational events at the Lilly Family School of Philanthropy, Indiana University–Purdue University, Indianapolis.

Leadership in Ministry
www.leadershipinministry.org
Articles, newsletter, and training programs for clergy.

The Western Pennsylvania Family Center
wpfc.net/
Offers many videos by Murray Bowen and a number by Edwin Friedman, available for borrowing by members.

Acknowledgments

I WANT TO THANK the many people who have taught me about money, beginning with my parents. Additionally, I want to thank my father, Howard Anderson, age 90, for continuing to ask me, "How's the book?"

I continue to be grateful for my mentors and colleagues in learning about Bowen family systems theory and applying it to my own life and ministry, especially Edwin Friedman, Larry Matthews, Jim Boyer, Elaine Boomer, Bob Dibble, and Israel Galindo.

I am grateful to those who read chapters or portions and gave me feedback: Howard Anderson (the "other Howard Anderson" who is not my father), Ed Bacon, Jim Boyer, Robert Creech, Randall Day, Morris Dirks, Heather Entrekin, Sean Harry, Meg Hess, Joe Kutter, Margaret Lewis, Phineas Marr, Laurel Neal, Joey Olson, John Rosenberg, Chris Roush, Jeff Savage, Jeff Sievert, Dee Dee Turlington, and Jeff Woods.

My terrific editors Cynthia Shattuck and Vicki Black once again provided wonderful feedback. My writing mentors and friends continue to support and encourage me, especially Jill Kelly and the parade of women who join her for Writing Fridays at her home and at writing retreats on Whidbey Island. Jill also sponsors a women and money group, which has helped me keep on track with my commitments to myself about money.

I want to thank Dave Ellis for teaching me so much about the value and pleasure of celebration. Thanks also to Bill Zuelke for introducing me to Dave's work and for helping me to lighten up about money (and many other things).

Thanks to my husband Karl for over thirty-three years of being my biggest fan, and for teaching me, among other things, that you don't have to order the cheapest item on the menu.